The Sacrifices of Men

Sequel to The Sins of Men

Danny J Bradbury

D1518241

Chapter 1

Peter Smith

Great News

The pain in my shoulder was acting up again. I stood up and stretched hoping to relieve my discomfort. I let out a muted groan. It's been months since I received the wounds in the battle against the crew of my old ship. The room started to spin as I'm overcome with a vision of being thrown across the gun deck and shattering my arm. My body shuddered from the memory. I still smelled the acrid odor of the gunpowder and heard the screams of wounded men. I doubted that I would ever escape the pain and the nightmares from that day. I stumbled over to the mirror that hung in our bedroom. All I saw was the haggard reflection of a tormented soul. I'm a young man who can't escape his past. There were dark circles around my dull gray eyes. My dirty blond hair hangs in threads touching my shoulder. I heard my wife calling. Time to prepare for my day.

I spent every day in this cramped office going over ledgers for the import business owned by my adoptive father and myself. All the while, my adopted country fought for its very survival against the might of the British Empire. I stood up to look out the window at the docks filled with ships. There was a calling from those ships that is hard to ignore. It's like the wail from the Sirens of Greek mythology whose calls are difficult to disregard.

"Son, are you well?"

I turned and looked at the concerned face of my father, John Smith. I owed so much to this man for saving me from the clutches of sailors off the British ship HMS Progress. I am forever in his debt. Holding up my right hand, "I'm fine. Just stiff from sitting too long."

He crossed the room and took a seat. I scanned his lined face. He was a tall man with sharp green eyes. His dark, gray-streaked hair was pulled tightly and tied by a black ribbon in the back. "We need to talk."

I returned to my desk and slumped into my chair.

"I know that you aren't happy working here. Your mind is always away on other matters. I see it also affects how you treat Anne."

I winced at the mention of my wife. "I haven't completed my duty. How can I be content to just sit here every day while we are at war?"

"Peter, you have sacrificed more than most men in the service of our country. What else is there for you to do?"

I absently stroked the nub that is what remains of my left arm. "Father, I know that I am a cripple, but I can't believe that there isn't a role that I can fulfill."

"Anne has told me about the dreams you have most every night. She is concerned about you, as am I."

I look down at the papers on my desk. "I believed that after I killed Captain Auger it would release my demons. It has not. I hated the British and I can't be free of the abuse that I suffered as a child until they are destroyed." My cheeks are flushed. I sat back to catch my breath and calm myself. "Did she also tell you that she is expecting?"

His mood changed in an instant. He blinked and rushed to my side. He put his hands on my shoulders and squeezed. "That is great news. Does your mother know?"

I shook my head as he ran out the door to share the news. How can we bring a child into the world during these times? I can't shake the melancholy that has overtaken me. It has seeped into every corner of my soul and won't give me any peace. I have to rediscover the joy that has escaped me since the day I started courting Anne.

I trudged in a daze through the bustling, crowded streets of Boston. The city was slowly recovering from the British occupation. Signs of that occupation are still present. The Boston Common greenery was returning to the grandeur that it was before hundreds of soldiers were camped there. I paused in front of the Old State House and focused at the square where the massacre took place. There were faint traces of blood embedded into the cobblestones. Shadows cast from the large building danced about the tiny square creating imagery of the deadly struggle of that fateful day. Such a waste of life. There was still fear among the townspeople that the soldiers could return. I saw it in their eyes. Walking on, I tried to avoid the gazes of the citizens who are both in awe of my celebrity and sympathetic to my war injuries. I rolled my eyes as I heard a child call out, "Mother, is that Peter Smith, the war hero?"

I don't feel like a hero. I was taken away from my family back in England as a young boy and forced to serve in the British Navy, where I was abused by a sadistic naval officer. I was able to escape the ship and was taken in by the Smiths. They embraced me and treated me as one of their own. I was loved and cared for, and raised under better circumstances than my pauper mother could have afforded. I learned the ins and outs of my adoptive father's business and was educated at Harvard College. During this time, which should have been the happiest of my life, I still suffered in silence from my abuses. I knew that the only way to exorcise my demons was to take vengeance against those who had wronged me. It was during the turbulent times in Boston that I was provided the opportunity. The mistreatment by the English Parliament passed laws to tax us and then sent an army meant to punish Boston were the catalyst that was needed for the revolution. I played my part, first in the militia in Lexington and then at the battle of Breed's Hill. Even with the death and destruction I witnessed and participated in, it wasn't enough to satiate my desire for revenge.

It was by chance that I volunteered to serve in the fledgling American Navy. This was to be my best chance to slay my past. During an engagement with my old ship, I confronted the man who took my innocence. I was enraged by the wrongs that had been wrought on me. I underwent an out-of-body experience leading American sailors aboard the Progress. I confronted and killed Captain Auger and we captured the ship. The look of pure horror on that evil man's face was eternally etched on my mind. What should have been the event that released me nearly ended my life. The injuries I sustained cost me my left arm and so much more. I was mustered out of the Navy and branded a hero.

I picked up the pace to get home to see Anne. She had been my only constant during this time. We met while I attended Harvard. A daughter of a local pastor, she opened up feelings in me that I had never felt before. I kept her at arm's length for so long and would not share my dark secrets. It was her sure will and love that kept me wanting a better life. I was a stronger man for it. She wanted desperately to have children and I should be happy for her. For us. How can I when there is so much still to be accomplished?

I turned down Beacon Street and stopped in front of our three-story brick home. This was one of the wealthiest areas of the city. The views of the harbor were magnificent. There was a deep-seated love that I have for ships and the sea. Still, I felt like a fraud to have been given this house by the "grateful citizens" of Massachusetts. The neighing of a horse caught my attention and I turned to see a carriage parked in front of the house. I mumbled. "The Proctors are here." I was never comfortable around Anne's father. She must have told them about the baby.

I took a deep breath and entered. The sitting room was filled with Anne's parents and mine. They were gushing all over Anne and she was soaking up the attention. Anne was a glowing beauty with tawny hair and soft brown eyes. She always took my breath away. I stood quietly until Anne noticed I'm home.

"Peter, I'm so glad that you are here." She ran to me and gave me a mischievous smile. Taking my right hand, she drug me towards our parents. The normally stoic Abraham Proctor patted me on the back.

"Congratulations are in order, Peter."

I attempted a grin but still didn't feel excited. Then I noticed Hester Proctor staring at me with tears in her almond-colored eyes. She was the epitome of a pastor's wife. Gray-haired and elegant, her dress was plain and drab yet regal. She was speechless but gave me a warm embrace. I noticed my mother waiting for her turn. She also had tears in her eyes. Amanda Smith was short and plump. Her blue eyes always conveyed a sense of sadness. We had much in common. I had to glance away so I wasn't overcome with emotion.

"Oh Peter, this is such wonderful news. Why didn't you tell me?" She reached for my arm.

I darted my eyes toward Anne. "We were waiting for the right time."

Anne must have sensed how uneasy I felt. "We should all go to the dining room and I will serve dinner."

Both sets of parents continued to chat but did as they were told. Anne lingered. "Are you alright Peter?"

I felt weak and sat down. She came and sat next to me. I tilted my head in her direction. "When should we tell them?"

She considered the question. "Why don't we let them enjoy the news of our baby first? Are you sure that this is something that you need to do?"

A part of me feels ashamed. I'm being selfish, but how can I ever be the man she needs if I am always unsettled? This is something that I have to do. "I am."

Chapter 2

Anne Smith

The Day Has Finally Come

This should have been the happiest time in my life. We were expecting our first child and it's been so nice having Peter home. Yet, I'm concerned about how troubled he was and the doubts he had about raising our child during a war. Peter had shared some of the horrors he experienced during his childhood and his time in the military. I hoped that he could put all that behind him. Still, a cloud of despair hung over our happy little family. I knew that he hasn't told me everything and the pull for him to return to the fight against the British was stronger than ever. I don't understand why he can't be happy here with me. Was it my place to stop him? I'm so conflicted.

I was raised in a strict and religious home. My father was a pastor who struggled to show me affection and expected perfection in everything I did. My mother was not strong enough to stand up to my father, but I knew that she loved me. It's challenging being a woman during this time. We lived at the whims of our fathers and then our husbands. I've always known that there was more for me and other women like me. My parents saw fit to let me be educated. I was forever grateful as this was not a common practice. It opened my eyes to the possibility for me to have more impact than my mother had. Before I met Peter, I even had dreams of having more control over my life. Maybe not needing a man to make my way. We deserved to have our voices heard. What better time than during a revolution for that to happen?

It may seem that by marrying Peter, I traded one man's home for another. However, I saw something different in Peter. He was sensitive and caring, and even though I made our courting difficult, he was patient with me. I was slow to forgive him for keeping his secrets from me about his childhood and the abuses he endured. He must truly have loved me to stand by me as I demanded his honesty. What troubled me was the change I saw in him when he returned from the battle that took his arm. He lost some of the spark I had seen in his eyes when we first met. I struggled with how I could help him get that spark back. Maybe it's something that only he could figure out. I'm so frightened that he will only be satisfied by going back to join the effort to defeat the British. Deep in my heart, I knew that he could be killed. Do I support him in that decision or do I stand my ground and make him stay with me and our unborn child? My intuition told me that I have to let him find the answers that he sought so that he can finally put his past behind him.

The day had finally come. Peter tossed and turned all night. I knew that he made his decision but struggled with the consequences. I quietly crept from our bedroom to make his breakfast. I started to suffer from bouts of nausea that my mother warned me about. I couldn't let him see me as weak. Today I would be supportive as I have exhausted all my attempts to make him stay. It's still dark out as I put the kettle on the fire to make coffee. I stood staring into the flames and wrapped a blanket around my shoulders. As the flames danced and the firewood crackles, I gasped when I saw images in the glowing fire depicting a great battle. There was a scene filled with hundreds of crazed men battered and clawed at each other in a desperate struggle. Peter was yelling and I didn't see what happened to him as a blanket of smoke covered my view.

A voice startled me back to reality.

"What are you doing, wife?"

I turned to see Peter. He had a look of concern on his face. My eyes rolled down to his feet where he had already packed his bags. "I suppose that you have made up your mind."

He stepped toward me. My first reaction was to back away, but I remembered my earlier decision to be supportive. He engulfed me in a hug and I melted into the cradle of his right arm.

He whispered. "This is something that I need to do."

Holding back tears, "I know."

He gently pushed me back at arm's length and stared into my eyes. He then kissed me on my forehead and knelt and kissed my belly. "I promise I shall return to you and your mother."

We ate without speaking. It was almost unbearable. He rose and grabbed his bag.

"I will write as often as I can. I meant what I said about returning."

I didn't dare tell him about my vision. "Be safe for your child."

He nodded and left. I cried for hours.

Chapter 3

Nigel Crittenden
Reporting For Duty

The wait was unbearable. I tried to maintain my composure. Military decorum had been drilled into me at the Royal Military Academy at Woolwich. Never show distress. I wondered what my father would think right now. His only son selected a career in the Army and did not follow in his footsteps to the Navy. I tried to recall an image of the man. He was away so much. It was hard for my mother to raise me by herself. She told me that I look just like him. Tall, with dark wavy hair and piercing green eyes. Now I only have memories of a man who died at the hands of a traitor. For the life of me, I will never be able to understand how a loyal British-born sailor could turn their back on his King and country to fight for the Americans. I had other plans in my life than a career in the military. I considered myself better suited for a life in the sciences where I yearned to understand the meanings behind the wonders of our natural world. I was engrossed in the teachings of Sir Issac Newton and Edmond Halley.

When my mother gave me the news of the HMS Progress's defeat at the hands of an American ship and an officer named Peter Smith, I made it my life's mission to avenge my father.

"Lieutenant Crittenden, General Pittman will see you now."

I looked up and saw a staff officer point toward a door. I stood and straightened my uniform. "Thank you, Major."

I confidently entered the cramped office and saw an elderly man dressed in a finely adorned red uniform. He had a stern look on his face. "Lieutenant Nigel Crittenden reporting for duty."

The General waved his hand toward a chair. He was reviewing some paperwork as I sat. It was stuffy and there was a musty smell of tobacco and outdated furniture. My eyes rolled around looking at the cramped office. There were no trappings that showed the service the general had provided. I thought the space wasn't worthy for a man in such a lofty position.

"I see that you just graduated from the academy at Woolwich. I also see that you requested an assignment for the Grenadiers. Wasn't your father a Naval officer?"

I sat straight as a board. "Yes, sir. He was killed in a naval battle in America."

The general sat back in his chair. "I'm aware. Why did you choose the Army over a career in the Navy?"

I blinked and clenched my fists. "I believe that I can make more of a difference in the Army, sir."

He nodded his head and looked down at the papers on his desk again. "I see that you are requesting duty in the Massachusetts colony." He looked up at me. "This wouldn't have anything to do with the American who killed your father?"

I fidgeted uncomfortably in my chair. "I would serve the Crown wherever I am sent, General."

"You shall get your chance. You have been ordered to sail to New York as a replacement officer in a regiment that has orders to capture the city of Charleston in the South Carolina colony." He stared at me waiting for a response. I nodded my head up and down. "Fine. See the major for your orders. You are dismissed."

I stood, saluted and left the room. I stopped outside of the General's office and tried to compose myself. I pulled at my collar. My mind raced. That didn't go as I planned. From what little information I could find, Smith lived in Cambridge near Boston. There was precious little known about Smith's appearance other than he was said to have lost his left arm in the battle. I needed to be sent to Boston to seek my vengeance against the man that caused my father's death.

I would have to adjust my plans. How far could it be from Charleston to Cambridge?

Chapter 4

Peter Smith

Where is General Washington

T he carriage ride was more comfortable and easier to manage than taking a horse. I had been on the Boston Post Road for two days and the landscape looked the same as it had when I took this journey a few years ago. A thick expanse of trees lined the edge of the dirt road which was narrow, only accommodating a single wagon in either direction. There were deep ruts cut into the road that at times were hard to navigate and were bone jarring. The road was populated with small villages left untouched by the war. The sky was filled with the sounds of chirping birds as they flitted around the trees. There was a chill in the air, and the leaves have started to turn to the rich fall colors of bright orange and burnt red. There was an audible crunch as the wagon rolled over the dead leaves littering the road. Billowy clouds floated in a bright blue sky like a fleet of ships skimming across a gentle flowing sea. There was little traffic which suited me just fine. Since the British Army relocated from Boston to New York, this area was virtually clear of redcoats. It seemed odd to have the roadway to myself. I snorted thinking about that prior trip to Philadelphia to plead my case to join the American Navy. This time I was headed to New

York to beg someone at General Washington's headquarters to let me back in the army.

I pulled my jacket tighter while trying to hold the reins with my knees. The isolation gave me time to reflect on the uncomfortable conversation that I had with both sets of parents. My father was more supportive of my decision, but my mother was mortified. She pleaded with me to stay home, especially since Anne carried our child. She blamed me for abandoning my family to go off and get killed in the war. How could she ever understand? At least Anne knew that this was something that I had to do. I made a promise to myself. Her parents said little, but Abraham threw daggers at me with his eyes.

Our farewell was brief and painful. Anne tried to hold back the tears. Still, they flowed. I think that she secretly believed the Army wouldn't take me back due to my injuries. Then I would return to her having gotten it out of my system. What was it about me that wouldn't allow me to forget my past and be present for my family?

I stopped in Andover to get some rest before the final push into New York. I took a room at the Daniel White Inn. It was a two-story, red wooden building near Hartford. I pursed my lips and nodded my head noting how secluded the establishment is. I avoided crowded boarding houses where I could be recognized. It's late afternoon when I entered the inn. The entrance was dimly lit and smoky from a roaring fire. I blinked as the smoke irritated my eyes. There was a scattering of guests eating in the dining room. I walked to the bar looking for the innkeeper and felt the familiar gaze of the patrons staring at the empty sleeve where my left arm should be. It was something that I never got used to.

"Can I help you, sir?"

I looked where the sound of the voice came from and saw an older man with a beer-stained apron carrying empty steins. "I need a room for the night."

The man smirked. "We have plenty of rooms available. Do you need some dinner and maybe a pint of ale?"

I looked over my shoulder and then leaned toward him. "That would be fine. I have a question."

The innkeeper glanced over my shoulder to see what I tried to see. He squinted and nodded his head. I knew that I was taking a risk. "Are you aware of any British soldiers in the area?"

He took a step back and scanned the room. I was suddenly afraid that this would blow up in my face. He grabbed my coat and guided me over to a secluded corner.

"You need to be careful who you ask that kind of question." He took a deep breath. "There are patrols that ride through here from time to time. What are you looking for?"

"I'm trying to find General Washington's headquarters."

The old man scratched his head. "Why would you be doing something so dangerous like that?"

I deflated. "I have my reasons."

"Well, young sir, Washington and his so-called Army skedaddled out of New York and are somewhere over in Pennsylvania. If you ask me, they are a defeated mob. If you can call them that. Do you still want the room and meal?"

I nodded and took out my purse to pay him.

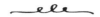

I woke up covered in sweat. Taking time to look around the unfamiliar room, I remembered where I was. I had my recurring nightmare of battling the British on that day that changed my life forever. I struggled to sit up and replayed the scene in my mind. It was uncanny how I could still smell the spent gunpowder and hear the screams from the wounded. The memory of my blood lust was frightening. I trembled as I remembered the moment when I reached Auger's cabin and ended his life.

I went to the stairs and stopped. I'm had doubts about finding Washington and pleading my case to be allowed back on active duty. What caused this sudden change of heart? It was maddening how often my mood changed. I had to be inflicted by some type of mental madness. I clenched my jaw and went downstairs. It was early and the sun was just rising over the horizon. The dining room was empty and I debated whether to eat or not.

"Good morning, sir. Can I get you some breakfast?"

I turned and saw the innkeeper. "Thank you. That would be fine." I watched him scurry away and took a seat at one of the empty tables. I scanned the deserted room and noticed a portrait of King George hanging on the wall. They must be hedging their bets. The innkeeper returned carrying a tray. He put down a bowl of porridge and a cup of coffee in front of me.

"I want to apologize for my actions last evening."

I stared at the man, not sure what he was talking about.

He must have noticed my confusion. "I should not have judged you for seeking out the Continentals. I have to be cautious. One never knows who they are talking to."

I smirked and nodded in agreement. "Do you know where General Washington's headquarters are?"

He sat down facing me. "From what I hear, they are constantly on the move with the lobster backs on their tail. Washington was able to escape with a good part of his army intact. The news isn't very inspiring. There are a lot of soldiers up and leaving the army."

I sat back in shock. "I had no idea it was going so poorly."

"Do you still want to find the general?"

I didn't answer the question and sat there.

"Then I would suggest staying clear of New York City. There are too many British soldiers and Tories there. Someone is bound to recognize you, Mr. Smith."

I was shocked again. "How did you know my name?"

He laughed. "You are well known in this part of the colonies. We have all heard the tales of your exploits against the British."

"So you think the Army is in Pennsylvania?"

"Either there or New Jersey."

I sat quietly thinking about my next move. I was too disturbed to eat. I stood up. "Thank you for the information."

He stood. "What will you do?"

"I will go find General Washington taking the direct route through New York."

Chapter 5

Nigel Crittenden

The Navy Waits For No Man

I took a deep breath and returned to the major for my orders. He ignored me and I cleared my throat. "Major, General Pittman commanded me to report to you for my orders."

He had a scowl on his face and reached for some papers. He stood and handed me my orders. "Lieutenant, you are to report to the 64th Regiment of Foot. They are presently camped near Portsmouth in preparation to sail to New York."

I took the documents and read over them. They didn't indicate how I was going to travel to Portsmouth. "Sir, how exactly do I get transport?"

The Major raised an eyebrow and gritted his teeth. He looked irritated and I went rigid awaiting a tongue-lashing.

He pointed out the grimy window to the street outside. "The regiment replacements are forming up to march the distance. You are to join your men." He squinted his eyes waiting for me to argue.

I came to attention and saluted. "Permission to be dismissed, sir."

He rolled his eyes and dismissed me by waving his hand.

I exited the stuffy building and looked around for the replacements. As I turned to my right, I noticed a long line of soldiers and wagons. I looked down to where my small chest of belongings lies. Picking it up, I hurried over to join them. When I got closer, a major on horseback called out. "Lieutenant, we have been waiting for you."

I struggled with my chest, "I'm sorry, sir. I just now received my orders."

He let out a sigh. "Sergeant Meadows, collect the Lieutenant's chest. We are behind schedule." He then glares at me. "What is your name?"

"It's Crittenden, sir."

"Well then, Lieutenant Crittenden, I'm Major Shenton. Join the other officers and we will be on our way. The Navy waits for no man."

I felt relieved to be joining the expedition. All those years at the military academy would finally pay off. This was the first part of my plan for revenge, getting passage to the colonies. I pictured in my mind the day when I met Peter Smith and ended his life. I smiled as I took my place in line with the other junior officers. There was a palpable feeling of resolve and a spirit of adventure in the task that we are undertaking. As we marched down the narrow road to Portsmouth, I gazed at the open countryside and noted the beauty of the rolling green fields. A brisk breeze rolled over the expanse and dark clouds drifted over our heads casting shadows over the scenery. In the distance, I spied an abandoned castle. I wondered about the history that has taken place there. Were there battles fought to defend this land from invaders? Small talk among the men can be heard above the clinking sound of the soldiers gear as they marched along mechanically. I turned toward another lieutenant walking next to me. He looked to be my age. I cleared my throat, "My name is Nigel Crittenden."

He had a confused look on his face but tipped his head. "I'm Percy Worthington. Nice to meet you, Nigel."

"Where are you from?"

Percy snorted. "I'm from Coventry, but I just graduated from Oxford."

"How did you come to be in the Army?"

He looked sideways at me. "My father is in Parliament and has connections. He explained to me that this is a splendid time to serve the King and ensure my future in politics."

We walked in silence for a few minutes. He then asked, "What's your story, Nigel?"

I raised my eyebrows. "I'm from Sheffield. I attended the Royal Military Academy at Woolwich."

"Is your father influential?"

I looked down at the dirt road as my boots kicked up dust. "He was a Naval officer."

Percy must not have sensed my pain. "Where is he stationed now?"

I nearly stopped marching. "He was killed in a battle with an American ship." I saw out of the corner of my eye that he wanted to say something but remained silent. Our conversation must have been heard by the others around us. There were a few grunts.

Major Shenton called out. "Best keep your breath men we have another thirty-five miles to go."

That suited me just fine.

Chapter 6

Peter Smith

Tories

The words from the innkeeper lingered. I made it a point to be more vigilant, on the lookout for any British patrols. I absently reached down and touched a loaded pistol I kept near me. There was a crispness in the air and I pulled my cloak tighter around my shoulders. I was getting adept at only using my right hand to hold the reins and adjust my coat. The farther south I traveled toward New Haven, the more traffic I encountered. I couldn't help but stare at each person I passed wondering what their intentions were. I thought about the real possibility that the innkeeper was correct in his warning to avoid New York. Was I being foolish or just naive thinking that I was immune to any danger in the heavily Loyalist city? I shrugged thinking about my last trip to New York. In the end, I decided to take the innkeeper's warning seriously and wouldn't cross the Long Island sound onto Manhattan. There was no reason to be careless at this juncture.

Once I entered the small village of New Haven, I decided to get a meal and rest the horse. I spotted a pub called the Sleepy Hare and pulled the carriage in front. A young lad, no older than twelve, took hold of the bridle.

"Sir, would you like me to feed your horse?"

I smiled at the boy. "That would be wonderful, young man." I threw my thumb over my shoulder. "How is the food here?"

He brightened up. "My Mum's the cook. It's the best meal in town."

I climbed down and patted his shoulder. "Well then, I'll have to see about that."

The pub was crowded and the patrons were boisterous. The room was dark and dingy, filled with smoke and the stale smell of tobacco. I wondered if there was some celebration that I wasn't aware of. A frazzled woman came my way.

"Are you here for a meal?"

"Yes, ma'am." I looked around for an empty table.

She wiped her forehead with the back of her hand. "Follow me."

She led me to a corner of the room and pointed to an empty chair. "I made a nice pot of stew. Do you need a pint of ale?"

"Just a cup of water, please. Is there a reason why everyone is so cheerful this early in the day?"

She narrowed her focus. "The good townspeople are celebrating the latest British victory over the rebels."

I let out an audible gasp.

She eyed me suspiciously and turned away stating, "I'll get your stew."

I sat there wondering what she meant. I hadn't heard about any recent battles. I got that uncomfortable feeling that I was being stared at. I looked around the crowded room and tried to listen to the conversations that were going on. I felt a chill run down my spine as I picked up bits and pieces of what the drunken revelers were saying.

"I hear tell that Washington's lads are on the run again." This was followed by laughter and the clashing of ale-filled mugs.

"Good riddance I say. This war can't get over fast enough to suit me."

Tories.

I jumped as the barmaid slammed down my meal in front of me. She narrowed her gaze. I watched her walk over to the celebrating sots. She was animated in her discussion and turned to point at me. The group surrounding her all turned in unison in my direction. I suddenly lost my appetite and stood to leave. A few of them headed toward me.

"Where are you headed off to?"

Sweat formed on my brow. How was I going to get out of this? "Gentlemen, I'm just trying to eat my dinner in peace."

One of the drunks snickered. "Did you hear that lads, he called us 'gentlemen.'"

They all broke out in laughter. I noticed one of them looking at my empty sleeve.

"What have we here? He's missing his arm."

I felt the blood rush to my cheeks. I left my pistol in the carriage and had no way to defend myself.

"You wouldn't happen to be a runaway from Washington's rabble would you?"

Just as my world seemed to be crashing around me, someone yelled. "What's all this about?"

I looked up and saw a large man carrying an ax handle.

"I'll have none of this in my establishment. Take it outside!"

I saw this as my cue to leave and headed swiftly for the door. My heart was pounding outside my chest when I went outside onto the road. I swiveled my head to see where my carriage was parked. At the same time, the pub door crashed open and the Tories flooded out onto the street. Out of the corner of my eye, I noticed the young boy waving his arms to get my attention. I stumbled in his direction while taking a glance over my shoulder to see that they were following me. The drunken fools seemed to be disoriented by the bright sunlight. I saw this as my chance and broke into a run. As I reached the carriage, I flipped a shilling to the boy and jumped into the seat, grabbing the reins. I shouted at the horse and snapped my wrist holding the reins. The horse jolted forward pulling the carriage. I chanced a look back and saw the mob running in my direction. I yelled out at the horse again and glanced down on the seat at the loaded pistol. Ever so slowly the carriage picked up speed and extended the distance from the crowd.

I knew by the look in those Tories' eyes, this wasn't over.

Chapter 7

Nigel Crittenden

Plan to Capture Charleston

My legs ached as we continued our march to Portsmouth. It was getting to be late in the day and the sun started to hang low in the western sky. There was an orange tint that glowed just above the tree line, and as I watched, melted into the trees. There was little chatter among the men and we settled into the rhythm of the hike to the coast. Just as I thought we would never get to our destination, we crested a rise in the road and spread out below was a vast Army camp. My mouth hung open while I took in the sight of thousands of the King's men camped on that hillside. The men around me reacted to the scene with uncontrolled amazement at such a sight. I couldn't contain myself. "Lord, that is truly a sight to see."

There were muted chuckles from my fellow officers. I blushed from my lack of decorum. A booming voice announced, "Gentlemen, see to your men. We shall camp here for the night. Tomorrow we will reach Portsmouth and load onto our transports."

I turned to the sound of the voice and saw that it came from Major Shenton. As the other officers went off to take charge, I stood there unsure what to do. The major dismounted and walked toward me. He glared at my inactivity. "What are you waiting for, Crittenden?"

I shied from his gaze. "Sir, what men do I see too?"

He took a deep breath through his nostrils. "Right. I suppose that I didn't tell you. You are to report to Captain Taylor. He is in charge of your company." He must have seen my confusion and pointed over my shoulder. I saluted and turned in the direction that he indicated. I waded through the mass of men who were going about setting up tents. I noticed an imposing figure watching the organized chaos unfolding in front of him. He wore the designation of a captain. He stood over six feet tall with broad shoulders and a ruggedly handsome face.

"Captain Taylor?"

He looked down at me, taking notice of me for the first time. "Yes. Who might you be?"

"Lieutenant Crittenden. I was told to report to you for my assignment."

He looked up and down appraising me. "I have been expecting you, Crittenden." He turned and started to walk away. He cocked his head to make sure I was following. "I have ordered Sergeant Clarke to organize the men into putting up the tents and seeing to the supplies."

We stopped in front of a neat row of white canvas tents being erected. I was impressed by the mechanical precision as the men went about their work. "How many men are in the company, sir?"

He seemed to consider the question. "Lieutenant, we have fifty men and officers. There are three other companies spread out in front of you. We are to be replacements for the losses that the Regiment sustained in America."

"I was told that we are to be part of an operation to capture Charleston."

He turned to look at me. "Who told you that?"

I took a step back from the force of his words. "General Pittman shared that with me when he gave me my orders."

He nodded. "We must be careful who we share that information with. There could be American spies who would love to learn of our intentions."

He slowly looked around him in all directions. I must admit that I was overtaken by his paranoia.

"Follow me."

We stepped into one of the raised tents. There were two small cots and a small desk set up. He closed the flap. "We are to sail to New York to join the rest of the Regiment, then on to take Charleston from the Colonials." He unfolded a map of the American coast. "We attempted to take Charleston early in the war but were repelled. This time we shall not underestimate the rebels." He pointed to the South Carolina colony and stabbed his finger at Charleston.

I waited for more, but he rolled up the map. I wondered how he knew so much. As he placed the map in a drawer, he asked, "How did you come about being in the Army? You don't strike me as the type."

I hid my anger from the slight. "I attended Woolwich where I received my officer training." He pursed his lips and seemed to be impressed. I continued. "My father was a Naval officer and was killed by the Americans." I clenched my fists and put them behind my back. "I felt it was my duty to serve the King and avenge his death."

That caught his attention. "What ship was your father on?"

"HMS Progress."

"I heard about that battle. It sounds like there were many mistakes made by the Captain."

I nodded my head.

"How do you plan on getting your revenge?"

My blood began to boil. "I plan on killing the coward who killed my father, Peter Smith!"

Chapter 8

Peter Smith

The Breaking Point

I kept the horse at a steady pace while periodically looking over my shoulder to ensure that I wasn't being followed. My mind raced as to where I should go next to find Washington's headquarters. There could be danger around every corner. All I knew was the Continental Army suffered another defeat, but where? For the first time since I left Cambridge, I was shaken by the events that took place with the Tories. Doubt crept back about my mission to rejoin the army. I felt like a selfish fool. This was an all too common experience for me. I was so sure when I left Boston and now I'm conflicted. I needed to make up my mind if I'm all in or not.

I spied a crossroad ahead and pulled the carriage off to the side. The Boston Post Road continued on to the southern tip of New York. The dirt path continued into an open hilly country with no cover. That direction would take me too close to the city and all the British soldiers and Tories. The other route, which disappeared into a thick covering of trees and brush, was marked by a crude wooden post with a sign that indicated "Albany Post Road." I was not familiar with this area and asking directions might be dangerous. I looked around. There was no one to get directions from anyway. The road went to the north which would take me away from the city, but how far would I need to go before I could travel west again? I took another glance over my shoulder and decided to take the safer route and turned the carriage to go north.

I've faced many situations where I felt alone and helpless; being a destitute child back in England, an abused cabin boy on a British warship, and fighting against hopeless odds against the might of the British military, but this was a different type of hopelessness. I abandoned my wife, who is carrying our first child, to run off on a fool's errand to chase demons that I continued to create. I jerked back on the reins and jumped down onto the road. I paced back and forth. When I couldn't stand it anymore, I fell to my knees, looked toward the heavens and screamed out, "What do you want from me?"

I sucked in some deep breaths of air and slowly calmed down. I reached my breaking point and came to the conclusion that I would turn around and go home. As I pulled myself off that dirt road, I heard the unmistakable sound of horse hooves beating against the ground. I stood in time to see two riders coming in my direction. I stumbled over to the carriage as one of the men shouted out, "There he is!"

I squinted against the sun's rays and the dust thrown in the air from the rushing horses to get a good look at my unexpected guests. I instantly recognized them from the pub back in New Haven. Instinctively, I reached up and grabbed the pistol off the seat, I turned to face them. The two men reined up a few yards away. "What do you gentlemen want?"

"Did you hear that Harry, he called us gentlemen again."

The other man chuckled. "Well, Angus, we need to show him how gentlemen treat traitors."

I felt the tension in the air. "I have no quarrel with you. Let me be on my way."

"It was Harry who figured out who you might be. A true hero for the cause, Mr. Smith. We wanted to find out how brave a hero you are."

"We thought we had lost you until we heard you let out that scream," the man named Angus said and reached into his jacket for a weapon.

A calmness overcame me and I turned and aimed my pistol in his direction. "You need to think about what you are planning to do." I saw a smile spread across his face as he pulled out his pistol. I squeezed the trigger and the explosion made my right arm jerk back. My visibility was obscured for a few seconds, but I saw the man fall out of his saddle and landed in a heap. I had all but forgotten about the other men when I heard the crash of a gunshot and felt soaring pain in my shoulder.

I turned to see the other man wide-eyed with terror and attempting to reload his weapon. I put the pistol under the remains of my left arm and reached into my jacket for my powder and musket balls. I had been under fire before and remained calm. I could tell that my nemesis had not. He spilled powder as he trembled trying to load his pistol. Time stood still as I took my time reloading and turned my gun on him. He looked at the end of the weapon, staring into that black hole, then looked into my eyes and started to speak when I pulled the trigger. The shot hit him above his right eye and he fell back onto the isolated road.

It was at this instant that I felt pain from my wound. I gingerly removed my jacket and saw a pool of blood spreading on the shirt which covered my left shoulder. I hissed while taking my shirt off and saw the wound. It wasn't as bad as I thought. I was fortunate that the ball passed through the muscle in my shoulder, missing any bones. I would need to get stitched up. I stuffed a rag over the wound and put my shirt and jacket back on.

I looked down at the men to ensure they were dead. There wasn't any traffic on the road, but that could change at any time. I thought about dragging the bodies off the road and trying to hide them but thought better of that. I guess that there was no turning back now.

I climbed up on the carriage and headed north.

Chapter 9

Anne Smith

No Word

I immersed myself into a strict routine while Peter was gone. I rose at the same time every morning and started into the chores keeping my large home tidy and in order. We couldn't afford hired help. I'm not sure that I would be comfortable having someone else do the work that I was certainly capable of doing. There was the added benefit of keeping my mind off worrying about my absent husband. I took walks in the park, weather permitting, to build my strength and maintain my sanity. I read books to sharpen my mind and newspapers to keep up with current events. There wasn't any relief from the nausea. It seemed like everything I ate upset my stomach. I wondered if this was a sign of how the baby would be. My mother suggested that I try chewing on mint to relieve my discomfort. I tried it with mixed results.

I came to rely on Peter's mother Amanda. She came and checked on me almost every day. She was a stronger woman than I realized. We shared our grief for Peter being away. Initially, I thought she was jealous of me taking away her son, but she surprised me. I looked forward to her daily visits. My mother, on the other hand, was mostly absent during the time I needed her the most. She blamed the need to help father with church matters and the distance from Cambridge to Boston as her excuse. I promised no matter what I would be involved in my child's life.

It had been weeks since Peter left. Still no word from him. I had no idea where he was so I couldn't send him letters. My daily routine helped somewhat with my longing to hear from him. While I scrubbed the pot I used to cook porridge in, I heard the front door open. Instantly a smile engulfed my face. Amanda is here.

"Anne, where are you?"

I put down the pot. "I'm in the kitchen."

She came in carrying packages.

"What have you brought me today?" I tried to sound upset about her gifts. The truth is that other than a small pension we received from Peter's service, I had little money coming in.

"It's nothing, Dear. Just some food I picked up from the market. I also found the loveliest dress at a shop in town. I instantly thought of you when I saw it."

"Mother Amanda, you shouldn't have."

"It's not much. John's business is doing so well, even with the war going on."

She started to unpack the groceries and without looking at me said, "Any word from Peter yet?"

I sat down at the kitchen table. "No word. It's been so long. Surely he would have written by now."

She walked over and took my hand. "You must be strong for the baby's sake. My son will write to you as soon as he is able. I also have not heard from him."

"Where do you think he is? He told me before he left that he had to find General Washington to receive permission to get back in the Army."

"There has been little news about the Army's whereabouts since they left Boston. John is working hard to procure supplies for the Army. I'll ask if he has any news about where they are located."

I put my head in my arms and started to cry. I could feel her take me in her arms.

"There, there child. I know Peter is safe. He loves you. He will write. Now let me make us some lunch."

Chapter 10

Nigel Crittenden

Portsmouth

W e were up before dawn. Captain Taylor and I stayed up late talking about the company and our shared experiences. He was from Staffordshire, where the regiment had been created. His father was a coal miner and the family was poor. Taylor wanted a different life and joined the Army during the Seven Years War. He fought against the French in Canada and distinguished himself by rising through the ranks.

I stepped out of the tent into the brisk, early morning air. The camp was coming to life and the men started to line up to get their morning ration of bread and a slice of ham. I needed a hot cup of tea and something to eat. As I looked around, I heard Captain Taylor behind me.

"Nothing like being with an Army on the move, eh Lieutenant?"

"It's quite a sight, sir. Where do we go to eat?"

He laughed. "It's this way."

We followed the other officers to a table set up with heaps of biscuits and meat. My attention was directed to the pots of tea. I could see the steam rising from the cups that had been poured. As I breathed in the bitter aroma of the tea and took a sip from my cup, Captain Taylor got my attention.

"Crittenden, come meet the other officers."

I grabbed a biscuit and dutifully walked over to the group of officers.

"Gentlemen, this is Lieutenant Crittenden, my new junior officer. Crittenden, this is Captain Arthur Nelson and Captain Orvil Johnson. Orvil is also a Woolwich graduate. You should have plenty to talk about."

Both men nodded their heads and I made a slight bow in return.

"Welcome, young Lieutenant. You came just in time to get into the action."

I took another sip of tea. "How much farther until we reach Portsmouth?"

A voice from behind me said, "It's another five miles, Lieutenant."

I turned and saw Major Shenton. He grinned sheepishly. "Gentlemen, let's get moving. See to your men."

I turned to follow Captain Taylor back to the company. He yelled out, "Sergeant Clarke, let's get packed up. Time to continue the march." Clarke moved off and started barking orders. I clung to Taylor as I was unsure of my role. He seemed not to notice.

In less than an hour, our three companies of men were back on the road just as the sun started to break over the horizon. The feel of the sun's rays on my face felt refreshing. I was in a grand mood and looked forward to reaching our destination and boarding the ship.

The closer we got to Portsmouth, the countryside was dotted with small hamlets populated by crude stone houses with thatched roofs. The people started to come out and greet us as we passed. The men seemed to be invigorated by the show of affection. I wondered how many times this scene played out throughout the history of the Empire. As we neared the coast, a brisk breeze rolled over us. I tried to see ahead for signs of the city and especially the fleet of ships that would be our transport to the new world.

Captain Taylor noticed me staring ahead. "Patience, Crittenden. You should enjoy your last few hours on dry land. The journey across the Atlantic is long and tedious. This time of year, the weather will be foul and the seas angry. There is little to do other than stay out of the way. I have made the trip several times and do not look forward to it."

I turned to look at him. "Why do you continue to serve?"

He averted my look. "This is my life and if the King orders me to go to war, I go."

His words took away some of the excitement I felt. We walked in silence for a while, then as we came over a rise, I saw the city sprawled out ahead. It was larger than I expected. There was an imposing structure near the bay that looked like an old castle. Beyond that, I saw a vast amount of sails from the ships anchored there.

"Your first time in Portsmouth?"

"Yes, sir. My father sailed from here often, but my mother and I stayed in Sheffield."

We marched down toward the docks passing through the narrow streets filled with filth. The odors were appalling. A mixture of human waste and the sweet smell of death and decay filled my nostrils. I also noticed several children who were dressed poorly and looked underfed. How could this happen anywhere in England?

"You get used to the smell and the poverty. Take care not to let the street urchins get too close. They will rob you of all your possessions."

I thought he was playing with me, but when I saw his expression I put my hand on my coin purse. We filtered down to the docks and I noticed more of the city's residents taking time to see us off. The town folks were subdued and watched more out of curiosity than patriotism. The men were lined up in front of the transport ships waiting for their turn to board. I continued to follow the captain as he watched the men climb the gangway. When the last of the soldiers had boarded, Sargent Clarke reported to us. "Sirs, the company is aboard and all accounted for."

"Very well, Sargent. We shall follow you aboard."

I walked up the wooden plank onto the ship that would be my home for the next three months. It was smaller than I thought. I hugged my shoulders considering spending months trapped on this ship with nowhere to go. I stayed on deck until the lines were cast and the ship was pulled out to sea. I stared off in the distance across the churning waters toward America. It was time to get on with this. I promised myself and my mother that I would find Peter Smith and end his life.

Chapter 11

Peter Smith

Recovering

I rode in silence enduring the pain in my shoulder. At first, I turned frequently to see if I was being followed. After a while, I accepted that it was clear of any more pursuers from the pub. While dealing with the pain, I remained mindful that I could run into a British patrol or more Tories at any time. I ran the encounter through my mind. Could I have avoided the confrontation with those men? Unlikely, as they were intent on pushing the issue. My celebrity had its drawbacks. Was it a sign for me to continue with my mission? I had almost turned around and went home before they attacked me. I cautiously lifted my jacket to check the wound. I winced at the pain that radiated from my shoulder. I hissed in a breath. The blood had stopped flowing, but I was weak. I needed to stop and rest.

The road snaked into and out of dense foliage. The afternoon sun cast ominous shadows on the path. A gentle breeze made the scene hypnotizing. I began to think I was hallucinating. Was my injury more life-threatening than I thought? I leaned forward and blinked looking at the path in front of me. My mind was telling me that a solitary rider was heading in my direction. I shook my head to try and clear my vision. When I still could see the man, I tensed up and reached for my pistol. When we were a few yards away, he called out to me.

"Greetings." He lifted his right hand to wave at me. I saw concern creep over his face. "Are you well?"

I pulled back on the reins and stopped the carriage. "Can you tell me where I am?"

He started to answer but must have noticed the blood on my jacket. "You need assistance. What happened to your shoulder?"

I glanced at the wound. "I had an accident. I'm well."

"If you don't mind me saying so, you don't look well."

I gave a slight grin. "Is there a town nearby where I can get a room for the night?"

The lone gentleman pointed over his shoulder. "Brewster is just around the corner. You can find lodging there. Do you need me to show you the way?"

"That's not necessary. Thank you for your kindness."

He hesitated then nodded and continued on his way. Part of me was concerned that the man would ride upon the dead ruffians and come back for more information. I couldn't be concerned with that and needed to get some food and sleep. Possibly medical attention too.

Just as the gentleman promised, around the curve in the road a small village spread out in front of me. Suspicious eyes followed me as I meandered down the narrow path that acted as a street. I called out to a group of boys, "Where is the Inn?"

They pointed down the lane in front of me. "Thank you."

A minute later, I pulled up in front of a dilapidated, two-story building that had a sign indicating 'Brewster Inn.' I was growing weaker by the minute and nearly passed out. Composing myself, I grabbed my bag, stuffed the pistol inside and cautiously climbed down. I struggled and stumbled at the front door. I was too embarrassed to see if anyone saw my weakness and entered the nearly abandoned establishment. I squinted against the darkness to see if anyone was there. Suddenly my legs gave out and I crashed to the floor. The last thing I remembered was being carried up some stairs and being placed on a bed.

"Mister, are you awake?"

The voice sounded syrupy and a great distance away. My eyelids fluttered as I tried to open them. As I turned toward the voice, a sharp pain in my shoulder stopped my movement.

"Is there anything I can get for you?"

It took great effort, but I attempted to open my eyes again. The face was fuzzy at first and I blinked repeatedly. Slowly, the face of a young woman came into focus. "Where am I?"

"Sir, you are at the Brewster Inn."

"How long have I been here?"

"You have been asleep for two days. We weren't sure if you were going to make it. You had a fever and yelled out in your sleep. The doctor came by and dressed your wound. We have tried to have you drink some broth, but you wouldn't take it."

"I'm thirsty. Can I have some water?" I watched her reach for a pitcher on the bedside table to pour me a cup. She helped me sit up and I took small sips of the water.

"I shall get my father and let him know you are awake."

I sat there trying to remember anything. I had a vague recall of getting into a fight with the two men from the pub. I realized that I could be in danger here. Panic nearly overcame me and I tried to get up. Still too weak to go anywhere, I collapsed back on the bed. I was resigned to face whatever fate would be mine. My eyes rolled around the small room. It was poorly lit and I couldn't tell what time of day it was. There was the rotting odor of death hanging in the air. I was well acquainted with that smell.

The door opened and I saw a large man, with a disheveled beard. He was wearing a stained apron that covered a huge belly.

"Well, well. Looks like you finally decided to wake up."

He had an angry scowl on his face. I braced myself. Before he could say anything else, I muttered, "I'm sorry to have put you out. I will be leaving as soon as I can get up."

His face melted into a grin and he pulled up a chair beside the bed. "You are welcome to stay here as long as you need, Mr. Smith."

I jumped at the sound of my name. "How do you know who I am?"

He reached over and patted me on my right arm. "I served in the fighting on Breed's Hill. I very much know who you are, Lieutenant." I looked at him waiting for more.

"I stayed with the Army for a little while after that, but it seemed so hopeless with each defeat and retreat away from the Redcoats."

I nodded my head in understanding.

"There have been some men looking for you. Something about two dead men back down the road from here."

My eyes betrayed my shock.

"We have kept you hidden. I also had your carriage and horse put up in the local stables. If you don't mind me asking, what are you doing in this god-forsaken part of the country?"

I averted his stare and muttered, "I couldn't sit home while fellow countrymen are dying to gain our independence." He looked away from me. "I'm trying to find General Washington's headquarters to see if he will take me back into the Army."

"Don't you think you've done enough?"

Why does everyone say that? I looked up and firmly shook my head. "Do you know where Washington is?"

He stood and started to pace the room. "All I know is they were whipped at Princeton by those lobster backs. I've heard rumors that they retreated into Pennsylvania." He walked back to the bed and with a grimace, said, "You might be too late. It's only a matter of time until the 'Continental Army' is destroyed."

"Surely you don't believe that?"

He slumped back into the chair. "I still want to believe in the cause, but it all seems so hopeless."

We sat in silence for a few minutes. "I don't want to put you and your family in peril. I will leave in the morning. Do you have any idea where I need to go to find Washington?"

He ran a hand through his unruly hair. "You need to get your strength back first. Let me try to find out exactly where the Army is." He stood up. "I'll get you a hot meal. I'll also have the doctor check on you again." He got to the door and turned back. "This village is loyal to the cause and the townsfolk will keep you protected."

I stayed in Brewster for another three days. Gradually, I regained most of my strength. I took daily walks among the residents of the tiny village. It seemed that they all knew what I had done in the war. I was surprised that word had traveled this far away. Maybe there was hope that we would prevail against the might of the King's military. We had to have a united front throughout all the colonies.

On the morning I departed, the whole village turned out. They saw that I was provisioned and the Innkeeper, Mr. Jacobs, found out the American Army had retreated to Morristown, New Jersey. He also came to learn that reports of a defeat were largely exaggerated. The Patriots had been victorious and drove the British Army back into New York. Jacobs sketched out a route that would take me around southern New York to cross into New Jersey. He warned me that many of the roads were no more than worn paths into the forest. He told me that I should avoid the main roads, which were still patrolled by the British.

I thanked him for his assistance and resumed my journey.

Chapter 12

Nigel Crittenden

At Sea

The transit across the Atlantic was just as I was told it would be. The accommodations were cramped and the food could only be called bland at best. I struggled to sleep in the crowded bowel of the ship. Between the stench of too many men stuffed together in a small space and the constant groan of the ship as it slashed through the Atlantic, I preferred being topside. The constantly rolling waves made most of the men incapacitated with nausea and vomiting. It made me wonder what my father saw in this kind of life. My memories of him were the tales he told me of his love of the sea. I spent time on deck watching the angry waters toss us around like a cork while I tried to recall anything about the man. My mother told me that I was born while he was away and had turned three before I met him. My earliest memories are of him being home when I was six or seven. He took me on a trip to London. Just the two of us. It was my first time in the grand city. I was in awe of the large buildings, filled with important people. He tried to explain the power that the city held. We saw that power displayed at the house of parliament and the Tower of London. These places held secrets of the horrors it took to maintain that power. I think that he tried to connect with me in his way. There was sadness in his eyes. I think he knew that he was to leave me again for his beloved life at sea.

It would never be the life for me. I preferred to be on firm ground. There was also the dull routine of trying to stay out of the crew's way while trying to keep the men in condition so that they would be ready to face the traitorous rebels. It was usually a futile attempt for the men to drill on a small moving deck while the frigid North Atlantic winds made our lives miserable.

With nothing to do to pass the time, I became more intimately acquainted with the other officers. I found that Orvil Johnson was a great role model and we shared stories about our time at Woolwich. He was a few years ahead of me, but we had many of the same instructors. We even endured the same types of hazing. The person I became closest to was Percy Worthington. Even though he came from a privileged background, I found him to be warm and approachable. We would spend hours talking about strategies that we thought would be successful against the amateurish rebels.

On a particularly cold night, I found him standing on the quarterdeck looking out at the bobbing lights of the other ships in the armada. I walked up and stood beside him. I could barely make out his features. There was a lit lantern hanging nearby and as it swung in the breeze, it cast off an eerie glow on his face. He appeared to be in a trance. I reached over and touched his shoulder. He was startled and jumped. He turned toward me and I could see an anger on his face that troubled me. Once he recognized me, his face softened.

"Nigel. I didn't see you standing there."

"Are you well, Percy?"

He shivered and wrapped his arms around his shoulders trying to beat away the chill in the air. "I haven't told you, but I have been to the colonies before."

I stood there waiting for more.

"I was part of the garrison stationed in Boston. My company was part of the regulars that assaulted the land mass the Americans called Breed's Hill."

I saw his eyes glaze over even with the absence of light.

"The men were enthusiastic to capture that position from the Yankees. We were very confident that they would not be able to stand up to the strength of our Army. We were selected to be in the first wave of the engagement. That was considered to be an honor. Little did we know that we were sent to our utter destruction. We had no idea that the Americans would fight so fiercely. We marched in precision and as we neared their earthworks, they released a deadly volley that punched holes in our lines. I sustained a serious wound to my leg." He reached down and massaged the area. "I fell to the ground and could only watch in horror as my men continued to their deaths."

I wanted terribly to reach out and take him in my arms. It just didn't seem like the right thing to do. "I had no idea, Percy."

He looked at me again. "I was fortunate to survive, and I was able to keep my leg. The surgeon said the musket ball barely missed the bone. They sent me home to recuperate. My father insisted that I not return. He didn't understand that I needed to finish what I started. So here I am."

I ruminated on his statement. Then scarcely above the din of the wind, I murmured, "My father was killed by the Rebels."

He narrowed his gaze. "Did you say your father was killed?"

I didn't make eye contact but shook my head. "He was a Naval officer. His ship, HMS Progress, was in a battle with an American ship. During the fight, he was killed. I have been unable to find out exactly what happened to him, but in reading published articles concerning the battle, a common name comes up. Peter Smith. Per these reports, he was a Naval officer who was English-born. He is credited with almost single-handedly capturing the Progress and killing a number of the crew. I have made it my life's mission to avenge my father's death."

Percy had a confused look on his face. "Why aren't you in the Navy?"

"I feel I have a better chance to find Smith on land."

"Well, we both have a reason to be in this fight."

After a grueling three months, land was spotted. It couldn't have come at a better time. We lost five men to either disease or accidents. When the call came that the coast was in sight, I hurried topside to get a good view. The rails were lined with soldiers and sailors. A haze covered the coast. I could barely make out the outline of the shoreline. I felt relieved at the thought of getting off this ship and standing on firm ground again. A Naval officer stood nearby. "Where are we going?"

He looked at me arrogantly. "We are to transit up the East River and dock in New York City."

I looked at the man with contempt. "General Pittman informed me that we were to capture Charleston in South Carolina."

He just shrugged his shoulders. "We all have orders to follow, Lieutenant."

I have to admit that I was surprised when I saw New York from the water. It was larger than I expected. We docked at the southern tip of the city. It was crowded with other ships disgorging troops sent to put down the rebellion. The sight was in contrast to the filth and poverty that I witnessed back in Portsmouth. Even the air was clear and fresh, which lifted my spirits after months spent on the ship.

"Gentlemen, go below and see to your men in preparation to debarking the ship."

I turned at the sound of the voice to see Captain Taylor. "Where are we to go, Captain?"

He smiled at me. "Lieutenant, we will camp on the outskirts of the city until the ships can take on provisions to take us the rest of the way to South Carolina."

I made a short bow to him. At least I had a better idea of what the plan was.

Chapter 13

Peter Smith

On to New Jersey

I followed the primitively sketched map I was provided. The one-lane path was nothing more than an old cattle trail cut into the dense woods. It led me on a northwesterly route. I knew this would keep me well north of New York City and hopefully the British Army. The downfall was that the route was claustrophobic from overgrown trees and lush undergrowth. I had to stop frequently to remove debris to move forward. While my intentions were pure to get back into the fight, I wondered why I faced hurdle after hurdle. To add to my misery, it started to rain. The cover on my carriage did little to protect me from the freezing downpour.

I'm not sure how long I endured the elements when I came to a large body of water. I studied the map, it had to be the Hudson River. I tried to look both ways and didn't see any signs of civilization. The overcast sky made it hard to determine how late it was. I somehow lost my pocket watch somewhere along the way. The river was flowing at a dangerous pace and I didn't see a bridge. It was getting dark. I didn't have the right provisions to camp. Should I chance going south along the river looking for shelter, or take the safer path going north? The misery of my soaked clothes made me decide to go south.

I must have traveled about thirty minutes along the uneven river bank when I came upon a rustic cabin. There didn't appear to be anyone inside. I called out loud enough to be heard above the pounding of the rainstorm. "Hello to anyone inside the building!" No response. I climbed down from the carriage and tried to open the front door. Unlocked. I peeked around the dark, one-room dwelling. It was indeed empty. There was a solitary bed in one corner. A few other items of furniture and some pots sat near a fireplace. It looked like someone lived there. I would take my chances. The first order of business was to light a fire and warm up. There was a small stack of wood piled next to the fireplace. My hand was shaking uncontrollably and it took an effort to get the fire started. The warmth from the fire felt intoxicating and I was mesmerized staring into the flames. Abruptly, my stomach started growling. How long has it been since I last ate? I reluctantly went out to the carriage to retrieve some of the dried beef that the townspeople of Brewster had given me. The rain still fell in sheets and I thought about my poor horse. She was feeding on some wild grass next to the cabin. There wasn't any shelter around to get her out of the elements. I did take the time to unhitch her and tied her up under the canopy of some trees and went back to the warm fire. I removed my clothes and hung them near the fireplace. Sometime, thereafter, I must have passed out from exhaustion.

I was startled awake the next morning with a musket poking my ribs.

"What are you doing in my home?"

I tried to see through the fog covering my eyes at the man who was threatening me. I held up my right arm and slowly sat up. The man was small and wiry. He had a menacing look on his face but backed up so I could sit on the edge of the bed.

"I didn't know anyone lived here. I needed to get out of the elements and stumbled upon your cabin."

He lowered the rifle and sat on a chair next to the bed. "One can never be too careful. There are many unsavory characters about these days."

I felt safer. "Do you live here by yourself?"

He snorted. "I'm the caretaker and operator of the raft that ferries people over the river. I was caught on the other side last night in the rain."

"It so happens that I need to cross over the river. My name is Peter." I held out my hand toward him. He looked at it and then reached out to shake it.

"They call me Andrew." He then noticed my empty sleeve and raised an eyebrow. "What happened to you?"

I wasn't sure how much I could trust my newfound friend. Cautiously, I muttered. "I lost my arm fighting the British."

"Is that so? That's fine by me. I'm no lover of King George."

My shoulders sagged and I let out a breath. "Well then, Andrew, maybe you can ferry me across the river and direct me to where I can find General Washington."

His expression changed to shock. "I don't support the King, but I'm not sure about Washington either. He has caused a lot of problems for those of us who haven't taken sides."

"Fair enough. How about taking me across and pointing out the direction I can take to keep me away from any British troops or loyalists."

He scratched his chin. "I can do that."

He helped me put the harness back on my horse and led me down to the river. I hadn't noticed the ropes that ran to the other side of the river and the raft that was attached. I was concerned about the length of the raft. "Will my carriage fit?"

He laughed. "I've taken bigger wagons than your little carriage."

The river overflowed its banks and ran swiftly due to last night's rain, so I was skeptical. When we reached the halfway point, I took a good look around. The clouds had given way to a bright, sunny morning. There was still a chill in the air, but the sight was breathtaking. It was populated with hardwoods whose leaves had changed colors to a deep red and yellow.

When we reached the far side I was able to breathe normally again. Andrew tied up the raft and turned to me. "You owe me a pound."

I did a double-take. "That seems steep for a ferry ride."

"I'm also charging for staying at my place last night."

I nodded and reached for my money purse. "Which way to the nearest town?"

He jerked his thumb over his shoulder to the south. "I don't recommend going there. They might not be as friendly as I am." He turned in the other direction and pointed. "You see that path right there?" I followed his finger. "If you go down that road, it will take you to New Jersey. You will have to ask around for Washington's whereabouts."

I traveled down that small path for hours. Then I came to a clearing and down below in an open valley I saw a small village spread out in front of me. I looked around for any telltale signs of British troops. It appeared to be clear. I rode into town and saw a sign proclaiming, "Fair Lawn." There was just a scattering of buildings and only a few people were seen moving around. I was committed now and entered the town. I came upon a woman who was dragging her child by the arm. I pulled up to her. I tipped my hat. "Madam, can I ask you where I am?"

She stopped and gave me an odd look. "Sir, you are in Fair Lawn."

I noticed that I had drawn the attention of other people. As a small crowd surrounded me, I began to think this was a bad idea. Then an older gentleman stepped forward. "What can we do for you, stranger?"

I didn't feel very welcome but had to ask. "I'm trying to find General Washington's headquarters and I was hoping you could give me directions."

He noticed my missing arm. "What would you be wanting the General for?"

I was offended by his tone and was tired of playing it safe. "That is between the General and me. Now can I get those directions?"

The man smirked. "Part of his Army came through here a few weeks ago. Said they were heading for Morristown. That would be about twenty-five miles that away." He pointed off to the southwest.

I looked that way and turned back to him. "Thank you, sir. I will be on my way." The gathered crowd stood silently watching me ride away.

Chapter 14

Nigel Crittenden

Finding a Ghost

Once the men disembarked and were assembled, we commenced our march through the streets of New York. As we strode up Queen Street, I was impressed by the wide cobblestone lanes lined with homes and businesses constructed of brick and stone. This was my first experience with the New World. I had assumed that it would be mostly rural and inhabited by farmers. The architecture was modern and vibrant. The tall steeples of various churches were visible. It was a city that could rival the majesty of London. New York was bustling with commerce and a strong British military presence was visible. I couldn't detect any obvious signs of the fighting that took place when the Army displaced Washington's forces. Had it not been for the strong contingent of us Regulars, it would be hard to know there was a war going on.

There was a large crowd that turned out to greet us. I was surprised by the reception. It felt like the greeting we got back in England. There were men, women and children yelling out greetings and waving the Union Jack. It was heartwarming to know that there were supporters of the King and his policies in the colonies. We went in a northerly direction putting the city behind us. We came onto an open plain with a clear view of the surrounding area. I saw cattle grazing in the fields.

Orders were barked out to set up camp. I followed Captain Taylor to direct the company to our designated area. As we watched the men go about the business of setting up their tents, I turned to the Captain.

"Sir, did the Major say how long we are to be camped here?"

He kept a watchful eye on the men. "He told me that we will be here for at least a week. That will allow us time to get the men back in shape by constantly drilling them." He then turned and looked around. "I would have rather gone straight to South Carolina and not have to wait. It will be hard on the men to have to get back on that crowded ship again."

I didn't respond but agreed with the sentiment.

We stayed encamped in that field for more than a week. Daily drilling removed the rust from the men after the long sea voyage. It allowed me the opportunity to practice leading the men. The military academy taught me lessons on how to lead men and maintain the proper decorum in a simulated arena. Now came the time to put the theories into reality. I was impressed by the discipline of the men but was careful not to cross the line between an officer and enlisted. It was ingrained in me to gain their respect, not their friendship.

During this time, we were also joined by the rest of the regiment. There was a growing sense of the importance of what we had been assigned to accomplish. We were told tales about the first unsuccessful attempt to capture Charleston. Lessons were learned about underestimating the colonists and their resolve. This time an overpowering force would be used against the defenders of the southern city. The overall plan was to split America in half and defeat the Continental Army piecemeal. It was inspiring to know that I would be taking part in this historic effort, but it did not detract from my original goal to seek out and kill Peter Smith.

I took a couple of trips into the city while we were in camp. I asked around at every pub and inn I came to for any word about Peter Smith. Most of the people I talked to had never heard of him. There was one pub I went into where I spied a solitary figure. The man looked to be a sailor by his manner of dress. I approached him and saw there was sadness in his eyes. The man looked to have had a hard life. I pitied him.

"Excuse me, can I ask you a question?"

He looked up at me. "You can buy me a pint and ask me anything you want."

I motioned to the barkeeper for two pints and took a seat. I could tell from his slurred speech that he already had too many pints. "I'm looking for some information about an American Naval officer. His name is Peter Smith. Have you heard of him?"

The man almost jumped out of his seat. He took another look at me and must have noticed my uniform for the first time.

"Lieutenant, why would you be looking for that man?"

I put both hands on the table and leaned toward him. "That man was responsible for the death of my father."

"Who was your father?"

I cocked my head, "Ambrose Crittenden. He was on HMS Progress."

"I knew your father well."

"How is that possible?"

He snickered in an eerie way that made me shiver. "I also served on that ship. I knew Smith when he was just a lad. He was the Captain's cabin boy."

I sat back in my chair. "How did you survive the battle?"

He bowed his head. "I was taken prisoner when the Americans captured the ship."

"Did you see what happened to my father?"

He shook his head slowly from side to side. "There was too much going on. I did see something that I will not forget for the rest of my life." He took a long draw from his pint of ale and wiped his mouth with his sleeve. "Your man, Smith. He was possessed as he came aboard the Progress. I could see that he was badly wounded, but he killed nearly every man in sight. It wasn't until after the battle ended that I knew who he was. He escaped the ship in Boston while he was still a young lad. I was one of the crew that was sent out to find him and bring him back to the Captain." He stopped and stared directly into my eyes. "The Captain was a very evil man. I was not sorry that Smith killed him."

"How is it that you are here?"

"The Americans released most of the crew soon after the battle. I had enough fighting and made my way down here."

I was troubled by what he told me. I didn't know what else to ask him. As I started to get up to leave, he reached out and grabbed my coat.

"That man Smith is a ghost and you should leave well enough alone."

I walked back to camp in a daze pondering what the old sailor told me. A small part of me wanted to feel sorry for Smith, but I still couldn't forgive him for what happened to my father. Either way, I would find him and kill him. Ghost or no ghost.

The day finally arrived when we were ordered to break camp and march back to the city. There was excitement in the camp as the men went about the business of taking down the tents and packing supplies with great gusto. We were addressed by General Pittman that morning. He told us the importance of our mission to defeat the rebels and end the war. While standing in formation listening to the General's words, I turned to Captain Taylor.

"How long will it take to sail to South Carolina?"

"It depends on the winds, but should only take a few days. Not months."

I smiled at that. I was conflicted about going south. It was vital that we defeat the rebels, but it would take me farther away from Smith.

Chapter 15

Peter Smith

General Washington

The weather turned for the worse and snow fell in buckets as I traveled down the rutted lanes toward New Jersey. Everything was covered in white. My hat and overcoat did little to prevent the flakes from sticking to me. I was miserable as the snowflakes melted and found their way down my neck and onto my back. I had to blink away the slush just to see the road in front of me. I longed for a warm fire to improve my mood. I couldn't move past the fact that I had already gone through so much to get to this point. It shouldn't be so challenging. On second thought, I snickered, setbacks seemed to follow me. At some point, I expected that the good Lord would see fit to make better accommodations for me. As I tried to huddle against the cold, my mind allowed me to think about Anne and our unborn child. Would I ever get to see them again? I haven't had the opportunity to write to her yet. She must be worried.

There had been little hope of me ever escaping the poverty that I was born into back in England. Then I was taken against my will to serve in the Navy and suffered abuse from the ship's captain. Then my life changed when I was taken in by the Smiths where I was loved and educated. I smiled at those memories of my time at Harvard and meeting Anne. Then

I recalled my timeline in joining the militia and battling the Redcoats at Lexington and Breed's Hill. My thoughts turned darker remembering my naval service and the epic battle against my old British ship. I thought that I had already lived a full lifetime of adventure. Yet here I was, in the middle of nowhere, in a blinding snowstorm looking for more trouble.

As the morning slipped into the afternoon, I was shivering uncontrollably. I hated to stop before reaching Washington's camp, but I didn't think I could make it much farther. I hadn't seen anyone else on the road to this point. I became more aware of my surroundings as I looked for somewhere to take shelter. The horse struggled to pull the carriage through the accumulated snow and had to be played out. The road I followed led me out of the woods into an open space. The snow was still impeding my vision, but I could faintly make out some buildings ahead. This lifted my spirits and I pleaded for the horse to pick up the pace. Just as I got a better view of the village ahead of me, two men stepped out from behind a tree and yelled out, "Halt!"

I had let my guard down and instantly regretted not being aware of the roadblock. I pulled back on the reins and tried to squint through the snowflakes to see who was blocking my way. Both men held muskets and were wrapped in rags. I could not determine if they were American or British.

One of the men stepped up to the carriage. "What are you doing out in weather like this?"

As I stared at the soldier, I knew I had two choices; I could lie, or I could take a chance and reveal myself. Neither of them struck me as King's men, so I replied, "I am looking for General Washington's headquarters and I was told it is in Morristown."

"Is that so? Why would you need to be seeing General Washington?"

I instantly felt a surge of relief come over me. "Soldier, I am Lieutenant Peter Smith and I need to speak with the General or his staff."

"Did you hear that Jonsey? We have an officer in front of us looking to talk to the General."

The other soldier chuckled out loud. "Well then, I suppose we should escort him there, Albert."

The man named Albert furrowed his brow. "How do we know you are who you say you are? I don't see you wearing a uniform."

I hadn't anticipated this happening. "If you allow me to reach into my bag, I can prove who I am." I started to reach for my bag, and out of the corner of my eye, I saw both men had raised their muskets.

"You wouldn't be reaching for a weapon, would you?"

I held my hand up. "If you will allow me to retrieve a letter out of my satchel, that will prove who I am."

Jonsey held his rifle on me and said, "Why don't you let Albert fetch that letter."

I moved over to allow him to climb up and snatched my travel bag. He opened it and pulled out my pistol. "Well, look what I found. You weren't planning on using this, were you?"

"Keep looking and you will find an envelope addressed to General Washington."

He looked at me with doubt on his face but continued to search until he pulled out the envelope. He handed it to Jonsey after he lowered his weapon. Jonsey inspected the envelope, "What's in here?"

I slowly put my arm down. "It's a letter from John Adams to General Washington asking him to let me back in the Army."

They looked at each other, then back at me. Albert took notice of my empty sleeve. "What happened to your arm?"

"I lost it in a battle with the British."

Jonsey looked confused. He handed the envelope back to me and started walking toward town. "Follow me."

I began to see the Army spread out in front of me camped at the edge of town. Fires were burning as the men tried to stay warm against the elements. Only a few of them paid any attention to me as I followed Jonsey in the carriage. When we reached a two-story, white building, I watched Jonsey approach some men who guarded the entrance. He pointed back at me and gestured with his arms. The guards looked at me and motioned for me to step down from the buggy.

I followed the sentry up to the entrance of the building. He spoke with the men guarding the doorway and they in turn opened the front door. I stepped into the grand mansion feeling the warmth of a large fire that radiated heat across the entire room. One of the guards pointed to a seat against a wall. "Wait there."

I sat grateful to be out of the cold. I looked around and did not recognize any of the faces that passed by me. I met General Washington after the battle at Breed's Hill. I wondered if he would remember me. As I started to get comfortable, I saw an officer head my way. I stood up as he neared.

"My name is Joseph Reed. I'm the General's aide. What business do you have with him?"

"Major, my name is Peter Smith. I was discharged from service after I received my wounds." He looked at my missing left arm. "I am healed and ready to resume my role in the Army. I have a letter from John Adams for the General to read." I held out the envelope.

He looked at my face as if trying to remember me and took the envelope. "Wait here."

I watched him step into another room. A minute later he motioned to follow him. I strode across the wooden floor dripping puddles of melted snow as I went. I cautiously entered the room. The space had been converted into a war room with maps strewn across a large table in the center of the room. It was crowded with officers of all ranks. I scanned the group and spotted the General. He was a tall man and easy to pick out.

Reed called out, "Smith, come with me."

He led me over to the General. I could see that Washington was reading the letter. I stood at attention in front of him.

He dropped the letter on the desk in front of him and looked up at me. "Lieutenant Smith, it's good to see you. How are you?"

I felt the stares from all the men in the room. "I am fit and ready to resume my duties, General."

The tall man smiled at me. "Mr. Adams has sent a very convincing letter to attest to that fact." He motioned to a seat and he sat down behind his desk and pointed at the letter. "He tells me that I should promote you to the rank of major and give you responsibilities in the Army training the men." He sat back and did not take his eyes off me. "I am very well aware of your record and valor. Haven't you already given enough to your country?"

Why must I always answer this question? I leaned forward. "General, as long as there are British soldiers in the colonies, I have not done all I can."

"Why not continue your service in the Navy?"

I sat up straight. "I feel that I can better serve the country in the Army. I fulfilled my mission by defeating my old ship and killing the captain. I have experience leading soldiers in battle and would like to put my efforts into that capacity. However, I can do more than just train as Mr. Adams suggests."

"We can never have enough experienced officers in the Army." Washington extolled a presence that few men could match. He got up and walked to the table with the maps. He looked over his shoulder at me and I got up and followed. He searched through the maps and pulled out the one he was looking for. "Smith, we have reason to believe that the British will emphasize taking the southern colonies under their control. I would like for you to take some men and go south to ensure that doesn't happen."

"Where would you like me to go, General?"

"Major." He said with a grin. "I believe that you will be needed in Charleston."

Chapter 16

Nigel Crittenden

Winter Camp

The camp was alive with rumors spreading like wildfire that we would be on the move. Officers of the regiment were called to assemble for a meeting with General Pittman. We had been camped outside of New York for a fortnight. Maybe we were finally getting orders to sail to Charleston. I followed the others to the Loyalist home used as headquarters by the General. There was some excited chatter along the way. A hand reached out and grabbed my arm.

"Nigel, do you suppose that we are finally leaving this place?"

I turned to see Arthur Nelson. "I have not heard any news. Only rumors, Arthur. What have you heard?"

He shrugged his shoulders. "I can't wait to leave this place and go somewhere warmer."

It was a chilly morning and a blanket of snow covered the ground. I blew into my cupped hands. "I agree, it would be nice to get away from here."

We gathered around the front of the house and stamped our feet to keep warm. After a few minutes, I could see Major Shenton exit the makeshift headquarters. He scanned the assembled officers and called out. "Gentlemen, show some decorum and come to attention."

We lined up in neat rows and stood at attention.

General Pittman came out on the landing of the house. He had a look of disgust on his face. This couldn't be good.

I could hear him clear his throat. "Gentlemen, I have called you together to provide an update on our orders."

I looked out both sides of my eyes to see the officers around me riveted by the General's words.

"There has been a change in our orders. Due to the rather disappointing results of the last encounter with the Rebels, General Cornwallis has ordered that we remain encamped here to add strength to the defenses around New York. He is concerned about Mr. Washington trying to retake the city."

There were some muffled moans.

The General held out his arms. "I am as disappointed as you are. I have arranged for building supplies to be provided to erect structures to house the men. It looks like we will be making our winter quarters here." He waited for any reaction. There was silence. "You are dismissed."

I honestly wasn't surprised by the announcement. The news wasn't as much of an issue for me as the others. My focus remained on finding Smith and exacting my revenge. If we stayed in New York, maybe there was a chance for us to go to Boston. I would have the rest of the winter to plan other opportunities for me to go to Cambridge and find the one-arm man.

We settled into a dull, mind-numbing existence in our winter camp. Passing the days with organized drilling and sending out scouting parties to keep the men occupied wasn't enough to prevent them from creating mischief. Soldiers weren't intended to be idle for weeks at a time. Many of them were the dregs of society taken from prisons across England. Counting on them to be outstanding loyal subjects was a fool's errand. We had to deal daily with drunkenness and fights among the men. There was also the occasional report of crimes against the local citizens that had to be dealt with. Justice was swift in most cases and punishment usually followed the severity of the crime. This could include confinement or flogging for minor offenses. For major offenses, the accused was subject to court-martial and more severe punishment. A case in point was the crime committed by a private named Johnson who was accused of raping and murdering a local maiden. I was assigned to sit on the panel that judged the young man. The details of the crime were gut-wrenching. A witness detailed the facts of the offense where the young private seemed to lose control of himself and brutally raped and beat the young woman to death. Johnson did not have any words to excuse his behavior. In the end, a hangman's rope meted out justice.

This wasn't the only issue that we faced during the long winter. Some of the men saw the opportunity to leave the army. They were aided by locals who were supporters of the rebel cause. They must have seen the chance to weaken the British Army by recruiting soldiers to desert. They would then assist these men to get away from New York and settle in different parts of the colonies. We tried our best to discourage this action, but even the threat of capital punishment didn't completely stop the practice.

My schooling at Woolwich did not prepare me for all that we faced that winter. It made me question my choice of career. I had yet to experience battle, but the thought of what that would be like was less challenging than time spent camped for months in this God-forsaken place. At least that's what I thought.

After months of sitting idle, we received orders to break camp and march with the rest of the army to capture the rebel capital of Philadelphia. This came down from the overall commanding general William Howe. General Howe saw this as an opportunity to end the rebellion in one swift move. Once again we were diverted from our original plan to capture Charleston. I learned to adjust to all these changes and accept it as life in the service. I was troubled that it would take me farther away from Peter Smith.

I noticed the mood of the men under my command as we marched back through the city. There was much chatter and laughter. To a man, the regiment was buoyed by the change in plans. Especially if it ended the war. There was spring in the step of the men as we marched back to New York City to board ships that will transport us to Philadelphia. This time, there was a lack of reception by the locals. Maybe we had overstayed our welcome.

Chapter 17

Peter Smith

General Greene

As so often happens in life, plans get changed. General Washington asked me to stay on while the Army went into its winter quarters. He reasoned that I could be useful in training the recruits who flocked to the Army after the triumphant battle at Princeton. It would have been difficult to say no to the General. He was a very persuasive man. I believed that I was fortunate just to be taken back into the Army and owed him.

Other than the blizzard that I endured finding the American camp, it was a milder winter than what I was accustomed to back in Massachusetts. The men didn't have the same viewpoint. I despaired as I wandered through the camp and witnessed them suffer from a lack of food and warm clothing. Another peril they faced was a disease that was rampant throughout the camp. This was escalated by constant weather changes from cold to warm, too many men in close proximity and poor hygiene. The "pox" was a horrendous disease that took anyone in its path. The pustules that invaded the body were painful and left scars if the victim was fortunate enough to survive the ordeal. I witnessed the ghastly effect the disease had on the men. General Washington ordered that the men be inoculated against the smallpox. This was a fairly new endeavor in which an infected sample of the disease was introduced into a healthy body through an incision. This was an advancement in fighting the disease and I was fascinated by the process. Most of the men weren't as convinced as I was. The prevailing hope was that it would save many lives.

My duties varied throughout the winter. I was assigned to a newly formed regiment from Massachusetts. This was deliberate as most of them knew who I was and were willing to follow my orders. Ensuring that they were properly provisioned was my biggest challenge. Even the basics of providing shelter and nourishment were dreadfully lacking. I wrote letters to my father, who worked for the government as an agent to supply the Army, begging for his assistance. His letters weren't as supportive as I had hoped. He wrote about his challenges obtaining supplies from our European allies. Mostly due to a blockade by the British Navy and threats of reprisals for any assistance given to our fledgling rebellion.

During this time, I also kept up a steady correspondence with Anne. She, in turn, sent me an abundance of letters. Her letters were upbeat detailing the progress of her pregnancy. I could detect an underlying notion of her concern for me. I could only guess how the separation was affecting her. It was only by sure will that I was able to stay at my post and not return to her arms. There have been many times throughout my young life when I doubted myself, but none more than this present moment. It made my mission all that more important to end this horrible war and get back to her.

As winter turned into spring, the camp came alive with activity. I got the sense that there was a renewed energy from the men with the turn to a warmer climate. Nature came alive from its winter nap with a rebirth of blossoming buds and the sweet fragrances of flowers. Flocks of geese added their echoing honks announcing their return. We were blessed with an abundance of wildlife that added to our rations. The men responded to this renewal which brightened everyone's spirits. It was time to get back to the serious business of defeating the British. I made it my mission to ensure that my men would be ready for anything that we may encounter. Supplies started to trickle into camp as the roads became more passable. This included weapons and ammunition. I instituted drilling to sharpen the skills that may have been lost over the long winter. I shared the lessons from the fight on Breed's Hill. I promised that we would never make the same mistakes that cost us that fight. We had every advantage that day; high ground, entrenched position and open fields of fire. What we didn't have was enough powder and musket balls to finish off the redcoats.

Throughout spring and summer, there was a period when each army felt the other out, but no major encounters. Word filtered through the ranks that the British were making plans to capture Philadelphia. I wondered how General Washington was able to receive such accurate intelligence about the enemy's troop movements. I was summoned to report to General Nathanael Greene for orders. I had never met the man. I heard that he was one of General Washington's closest advisors. Upon entering his tent, I was struck by his presence. He was a handsome man with a serious gaze and an air of authority about him. I heard that he was a Quaker from Rhode Island. How he must be conflicted about war and killing. He looked up from his desk and instantly broke into a smile.

"Major Smith, reporting as ordered."

He rose and came to me with his arm stretched out. As I took his hand in mine, I noticed a noticeable limp. I also saw him stare at my empty sleeve.

"Major, it's so good to finally meet you. I have heard many great things about you. Please have a seat." He pointed to an empty camp chair. "I have asked you here to give you your orders. Your company has been attached to my command and you will report directly to me." He leaned closer. "General Washington has spies everywhere. They have detected a plan by General Howe to capture our capital. It will be our job to make sure that Lord Howe fails."

I shared the news with the men of the impending British invasion of Philadelphia. I could see on their faces that they understood the importance of our mission to prevent that from happening. I made sure that they understood our priority was to defeat the Redcoats and drive them off the continent. They responded with a resounding cheer. I knew these men would follow me to hell and back.

There was an element of resolve as we marched into Pennsylvania for our engagement with the enemy. It was a warm, early September day. The countryside was still and we were covered by a canopy of trees along our path. I strolled among the men listening to their conversations. I sensed an excitement to be on the move again. There was a power that could be felt from an army on the move. Still, there was an underlying fear of the unknown that the men experienced before a battle.

When we reached Brandywine Creek, we were sent to the left flank of the American line. According to General Greene, we were laying a trap to funnel the British into the center of our lines and destroy them. There was a dense fog lifting off the cool water of the creek which spread its tentacles toward us. It was an eerie sight and prevented a clear view of the other side of the stream. It made me think back to my childhood in England experiencing the coastal fog. I wasn't sure if it was an omen for the battle to come.

We took our place near the creek and waited for the enemy.

Chapter 18

Anne Smith

At Last

After weeks of endless longing, I finally received a packet of letters from Peter. My pulse beat uncontrollably as I read through each letter. The letters were upbeat. They chronicled his journey to New Jersey. There was no mention of struggles. He made it sound like a leisurely walk through the park. I immediately saw through them. At least I knew he was still alive. He mentioned meeting with General Washington and being admitted back into the Army with a promotion to major. I reread each letter. No mention of where he would be sent. As I put the letters down, I felt the baby move. He or she must be just as excited as I was to hear from their father.

I don't know whether I should be relieved or worried by the tone of the letters. I started to get up when the front door crashed open.

Amanda had a wild look in her eyes. She held out a stack of letters. "Anne, did you hear from Peter!"

I couldn't help myself and I started laughing. She tilted her head and looked like I offended her. I covered my mouth and when the giggles were under control, I held up my letters and said, "I just received a packet of letters."

She stormed over to the table and plopped down in a chair. "What did he say?"

I waited until she caught her breath. I shrugged my shoulders. "Not much specific to where he was. He met with Washington and was admitted back into the Army. He did mention that they are in their winter camp. The letters are upbeat and make it sound like he is safe."

Amanda leaned toward me. "Sounds like the same thing he wrote to me. I don't know whether to be concerned or not."

"I will be concerned until he comes home."

With the coming of spring and the much-needed warmer weather, I extended my daily walks. The baby had grown and my stomach swelled. He or she was very active. It should be only a few more weeks until I deliver. Part of me was excited, but I wished that Peter could be here to experience the birth. I am troubled by my dreams which continually portend tragedy for Peter. Today I will go to the church and speak with my father.

I entered the empty meeting house. I spent many days in this place, worshiping a benevolent God. I never had doubts about him protecting me, but all the current events have made me skeptical. Dust dances through the sunlight that shines through the windows and there is a musty smell in the empty chapel. I strolled to the back of the church touching the back of the pews as I passed. I saw a faint light in my father's study. I peeked into the small office which is cluttered with books. Pastor Proctor is hunched over scribbling what I assumed was this week's sermon. I have always admired the man for his convictions. "Ahem, Father, do you have time to talk?"

He nearly jumped out of his seat. "Anne, is everything okay?"

"Can I sit?"

He stood up and pulled out a chair for me.

"How is the baby?"

I absently rubbed my stomach and smiled at him. "Very active."

He sat on the edge of his desk. "What can I do for you?"

"I have been having troubling dreams about Peter."

He waited for more.

"In these dreams, something terrible happens to him."

He shook his head slightly. "It's normal for you to be concerned about his safety. He is in a dangerous position. Added to this stress, you are carrying your first child." He pointed at the baby. "Have you continued your prayers?"

I had tears in my eyes. "Yes, Father, I pray every day. I want to know that God is hearing me and will protect Peter and send him home to me."

He did something that he rarely did. He reached out and patted me on the shoulder.

"God has a plan for all of us. We must trust in his plan and be faithful to him."

I knew that his words should have been comforting to me, but I felt more depressed. We chatted for a little while longer, then I excused myself.

The walk back home was difficult. I had to stop and rest. It wasn't good for the baby with my state of mind. I needed to go and see my husband. How could I make that happen before the baby came?

Chapter 19

Nigel Crittenden

On to Philadelphia

We languished for a month on that ship before finally being able to go ashore in Maryland. It was painful to be so close to land but made to stay aboard that cramped transport waiting to be back on firm ground. I never learned why we had to stay at sea as long as we did. It was another blow to the morale of the men who had already endured so much during our stay in New York. It felt comforting to be back on land. There were rumors abound that a few dozen men perished during the journey south. It took hours to disembark the thousands of troops under General Howe's command. We were ordered to make camp on the west side of the Elk River across from Pennsylvania. It was early September and the weather was uncomfortably hot. My uniform was made from wool which supposedly allowed for one to remain cool. However, due to the layers of clothing I wore, it retained my sweat, especially in warmer months. It made for a miserable experience, especially on long marches.

We stayed in camp for a week to rest up and heal from the excursion from New York. I deliberately walked through camp to get a sense of the mood of the men. As they still didn't know me, their reactions were guarded to my questions. I saw resolve in those untrusting eyes. For many of them, this would be their first test under fire. This included me. After the week's rest, we were directed by General Howe to commence our march to Philadelphia to capture the rebel capital. I watched with pride as the men took to the march. Our vast numbers snaked along the rural dirt paths through southern Pennsylvania. We were met by a few of the locals along the way. There were cheers from those I assumed were loyal to our cause, but there were also hateful stares from those who looked at us as invaders. If all these colonists became united in their desire to break away from the British Empire, it could be difficult to defeat them. It was comforting to see that hadn't been the case. I wondered if the disloyal citizens were reporting out movements to the rebels. It would be hard to hide this many men.

Our superiors directed us to push the men. They didn't explain the sense of urgency. I assumed that we would easily overpower any force in our way guarding Philadelphia. These Americans were foolish people. How could they possibly stand up to the strength of the British Army? As I marched along with the men, my thoughts turned back to my purpose of being here. I wondered where my sworn enemy Peter Smith was at that time. It would seem that I was even further away from him. It didn't deter me from somehow finding him and exacting my revenge for the death of my father. Still, there were times like now when I would forget about Smith. This concerned me. I felt pangs of guilt for my mother and especially my father if I couldn't complete my task. I couldn't ever forget the reason I was here.

We pushed on through the night and had to be near our objective. I was exhausted from hours on the road. The men, to their credit, kept any display of discomfort to themselves. As we halted, there was nervous murmuring in the ranks. In the predawn hours, it was hard to make out our surroundings. There was some commotion ahead and I stepped out of formation. I strained my neck to get a better look. There was the chatter of voices and I turned my head in that direction. I could hear excited men calling out orders. I broke the ranks to go ahead and investigate. As I stumbled in the dark, I was confronted by Captain Taylor.

His voice was high-pitched. "Crittenden. We have word that the Rebels are entrenched ahead waiting for our arrival. A local scout has provided the location of the enemy and is to show us a way to flank Washington's Army. Go back to your men and prepare them to march quickly."

My heart pounded uncontrollably as I made my way back. The time has come to show what I am made of. I was out of breath when I reached the men. I was gasping for air. "The enemy has been spotted ahead and we are to cross the stream and strike them on their right flank."

It was difficult to see each man's face, but I could hear in their voices they were excited. I turned at the sound of orders being barked out along the line. "Here we go, men. Follow me."

Chapter 20

Peter Smith

Hold Steady

The air was thick with a blanket of tension along with the fog that covered our front. We waited patiently for the redcoats to show themselves. We were placed away from the creek and anchored to companies of our fellow countrymen on both sides. I watched with amazement as cannons were brought up and made ready to fire. As the sun crested the tree line, I saw ribbons of crimson which spread out in the morning sky. Would that portend the battle that was to come. The veil of fog started to lift off the water and I saw the outline of troops in the distance. I took a position in front of my assembled troops. My gaze shifted around at the men and saw the fear on their faces. I wondered how many of them had not experienced battle yet. I was transported back to my first encounter at Lexington. I shook my head. No time to daydream.

With a strong voice, I called out. "Hold steady, men. We have the advantage. They will regret facing us this fine morning." I watched as some of the tension drained from their faces. I swelled with pride. This would be more glorious than the stand we made at Breed's Hill and we were better prepared.

With the lifting of the fog, we had a clearer picture of what soldiers were deployed in the heights across from us. I saw the unmistakably pointed helmet of Hessian soldiers. I had yet to face these mercenaries, but I was familiar with their legend of ruthless fighting. I strained my neck to try and see where the bulk of the English were. Something didn't seem right. The Hessians weren't making any aggressive movements. Could this be a diversion? I scrambled back behind the ranks to get an update from someone in command. As I scanned for General Greene, the air was suddenly filled with the sound of cannon fire. I turned back to see the crashing of shells being lobbed at the enemy. The smell of spent powder was thick and took me instantly back to the battle at sea with the British ship Progress. I strained to look through the shroud of smoke to see if the cannonade was having any effect, and then the British guns opened up. Through all this, the Hessians remained stationary. How odd.

I continued my search for orders when I spotted General Greene in a heated conversation with an aide. He quickly looked across the creek and his face contorted into a scowl. He turned in my direction and pointed at me. "Major Smith, go back and gather your company. We are being outflanked to the north."

We both turned to the sound of gunfire in that direction.

"Now, Major!"

I ran back and started shouting orders. "Men. Our right flank is being turned and we are ordered to prevent the British from destroying our Army. Gather your weapons and follow me." I didn't turn to see if they were following. We got in line behind other companies of Continental soldiers heading north on a narrow path through thick vegetation. The closer we got, the more I could see that the redcoats were trying to breach a gap in the American lines. I grabbed my sword and started to wave it over my head. "This way, men. We have to plug the line."

We made a mad dash to the opening. As men began to fall around me with ghastly wounds, I halted the company. "Form a firing line right here." I anxiously watched the men form two lines. I took my place behind the line. "Take aim." Dozens of muskets came up toward the mass of redcoats streaming in our direction.

"Fire!"

The thunder of musket fire was deafening. A thick cloud of smoke covered our front. The smell of sulfur was somehow comforting. The men automatically reloaded their muskets as I stared out to see the effect of our volley. I blanked out everything around me as I stood waiting for the British to pour into our lines. Then as the smoke lifted, I saw that the ground was littered with dead and wounded red-coated soldiers. Sadly, I was immune to such sights and turned my attention to the gap in our lines. I looked across the body-strewn field in front of me and could see the British had reformed for another attack.

Chapter 21

Nigel Crittenden

Fix Bayonets

T he sound of distant cannon fire could be heard. Onward we marched. We waded across the creek which was covered by a thick fog that sat idly covering the stream. The water was colder than I expected. A shock to the system. The sun glowed red and could be seen breaking through the thick growth of trees along the bank of the water. The troops were well disciplined and remained stoic yet determined throughout the march. My thoughts turned to my training at Woolwich. Never let the men see you panic. I was filled with excitement, but there was an underlying fear of the unknown. Would we truly catch the Americans off guard?

We moved rapidly through the morning hours undetected. I wasn't informed of how far that we had to go to reach the flank of the Americans. The men kept up a steady pace along with the thousands of their fellow soldiers. Under no circumstances would the Rebels be able to overcome the force that was coming their way. As the sun rose in the sky, we continued toward our destination. There didn't seem to be a slackening of cannon fire downstream. I wondered how that battle was progressing.

We finally reached an open field. Up ahead the first regiments of His Majesty's troops were engaging the Rebels. I watched the Americans recoil from the initial assault. The men around me let out shouts of joy at the sight. We picked up our pace toward a large gap in the enemy's lines. A fool could see that we would easily carry the day. Orders were given to spread out in a battle line and cut through the American resistance.

Just as we reached the weakening line of the enemy, reinforcements came from nowhere. How could this be? Major Shenton shouted orders to halt and send a volley into the Rebel line. I eyed Sergeant Clarke move in front of the line to straighten it up for the volley. I followed his example and pulled out my sword and positioned myself behind my company of men. Everyone moved mechanically as the men had been trained. They calmly took their place and awaited orders. Down the line the order, "Make ready," was given. The men in unison cocked their rifles and planted their feet. Then came the order, "Present." Each man brought the butt of their weapon up to their shoulder and aimed. After a few seconds, "Fire!" Hundreds of muskets discharged simultaneously, and when the smoke cleared, holes could be seen punched in the American lines.

The order to fix bayonets was followed by "Advance." The massed lines began to move forward at a steady pace. I felt a surge of energy as we would now finish the Colonials off. Then to my horror, another line of Americans formed and were preparing to fire upon my men. I tensed and gripped my sword tighter awaiting the volley. I didn't have to wait long. The explosion from the enemy muskets devastated the ranks of British soldiers. I heard musket balls wiz near my head and instinctively ducked. I wasn't prepared for the number of men who fell, lying dead and dying on the ground at my feet. I couldn't take my eyes off one of the men who had been shot in his neck. He grasped his wound with both hands and stared at me as the life drained out of him.

The order was given to fall back and reorganize. The men who could still fight began to slowly back away from the Americans. I kept an eye on the Rebels to ensure that they were not following and joined my men.

What looked like a rout turned into a stalemate with each side trading volleys. The fighting was desperate at times with the lines of men close together. This resulted in hand-to-hand clashes and the shifting of the forces along the length of the battlefield. The screams of dying men mixed with the shouts of those who were frenzied acting in self-preservation. The Americans fought valiantly to stave off being overrun by our superior forces. As the fighting raged, I took notice of a Rebel officer who stood calmly directing his soldiers. Through the haze of battle, I focused on him. The man walked among his company guiding them always in the right place to repel our advances. Even though he was my enemy, I grew to admire his bravery. The man was missing his left arm. My mind was exhausted from battle, but it tried to warn me that this was important.

Chapter 22

Peter Smith

Retreat

I remained calm, calling out orders to my men. They needed to see me as a steadying influence so they could perform their deadly work. At times, it was a hopeless struggle to prevent the British from overrunning our position. I feared a repeat of Breed's Hill, as the Redcoats came at us with bayonets. The men held their ground and refused to retreat. This time we had enough ammunition to keep them at bay. Through the fog of the battle, I witnessed desperate moments when the fighting became personal and both sides grappled with each other. The killing and maiming was horrific. Men were using their fists or any weapon within reach to dispatch their foes. It reminded me of the horrors I experienced battling the English sailors on the Progress. I decided that maybe I wasn't completely immune to the death of so many. I hoped for the sake of my soul that I never would be.

We struggled for hours holding out hope that we would receive reinforcements to turn the tide. They never came. As darkness crept over the battlefield, both sides showed signs of being played out. We were ordered to abandon the field. I knew that the men were as exhausted as I was. There was only sporadic gunfire and the moans of the wounded could be heard. It was against everything that I stood for to leave the field to the British and to forsake our wounded men to be captured by the enemy. Still, we needed to remain intact to continue the fight. Begrudgingly, I walked among the men and in a hushed tone, "Men, you have acted bravely and given everything you have. It is time for us to take leave and live to fight another day."

I saw the disappointment on their faces as they got up from their positions and retreated into the darkness of the night.

The men were subdued and quiet on the march away from Brandywine Creek. I wanted to lift their spirits, but I knew from experience that they had to deal with their demons in their way. I was desperate to know how heavy our casualties were. Would we be fit enough to put up a defense if the British decided to pursue us? They had to be just as exhausted and bloodied as we are.

Once we reached the relative safety of Chester, I was able to reflect on the day's events. As always happened, I was immersed in self-doubt. I wondered if there was anything that I could have done differently to change the results. Then, as a blanket of fog overcame my mind, I thought about Anne and our unborn child. I had not written a letter in over a week and had no news of them. I fell back into questioning the merits of going through all this again. I tried to convince myself that I was fighting for their future, but I was just being selfish. This was not the time to make any rash decisions. I got up to check on the men. Tomorrow would be a new day.

Chapter 23

Nigel Crittenden

Rebels in Retreat

As darkness descended over the landscape, I knew the fight was essentially over. I scanned the ground in front of me littered with the dead and dying. The creeping shadows from the last rays of the sun lit a ghastly glow on the heaps of men scattered on the bloody ground. It was a sight that I shall never forget. Major Shenton found me. There was a possessed look on his face. "Crittenden, why have you halted the advance?"

I couldn't take my eyes off his face. What had overcome him? "Sir, the men are played out. We have taken a ghastly number of casualties."

The Major looked around at the men. Most of them had collapsed on the ground, many with wounds from the intense fight. He began to pace and then turned sharply toward me. "Don't you see, man. We can finish them off today." He stared right through me.

I stood there with a blank expression on my face. It must have convinced him to think about what he was ordering. His eyes rolled over the field. I watched as his face registered a clear picture of where things stood. Still, orders were orders. He stood ramrod straight. "Lieutenant, organize your men for another attack."

The other surviving officers and I barked out orders for the men to reform for another charge. The men reluctantly fell into a ragged line preparing themselves for more horror.

We stepped off at a slow pace, careful to step over the bodies of our comrades. It was hard to make out the outline of the Rebel forces as darkness descended. As we continued our advance, there was no opposition. It soon became apparent that the enemy left the field. There was a hushed celebration among the men. We had won the day, but where were the Americans? I looked for Sergeant Clarke. He was in position behind the front line.

"Sergeant Clarke, take a squad of men forward to ensure that the Rebels have retreated."

He snapped to attention. "Sir." He moved along the men, grabbing a few of them and leading them into the darkness. I watched them fade into the night, listening for any sign of an ambush. After a few harrowing minutes, a solitary shadow moved slowly back toward the line.

"Lieutenant, Sergeant Clarke sent me back to tell you that the enemy has completely abandoned the field."

I let out a breath. "Very well." I turned to the soldier standing next to me. "Private Shipley, find Major Shenton and report that the Americans have surrendered the field to us and I await his orders."

Orders came back to set up camp for the night and tend to the wounded. It had been a costly day and we allowed the Rebels to escape. The war would continue, but for how long? Would I ever find Smith?

I rose early the next morning and tried to stretch my aching muscles. I pulled open my uniform and tried to feel for any telltale signs of wounds.

I pulled out my hand. No blood. It was only by divine intervention that I wasn't hit by all those musket balls. Still, the fighting took its toll on me. I would forever be changed by the experience.

The camp became alive with activity. I could smell breakfast being cooked and my stomach rumbled. As the sun crept over the treeline, I walked among the men and a clearer picture formed in my mind. What should have been a magnificent rout turned into a battle of stalemate. The men were mumbling about the incompetence of the officer corp in allowing the Rebels to escape to fight another day. I allowed them to voice their opinions. Maybe they are right.

I was thinking too much. It wasn't my role to question orders. There were plenty of mistakes made, but for my first fight, I made a good showing of myself. I stood up to the best the enemy could throw at us and I stood my ground. Something was troubling me. I couldn't put my finger on what. While I was in a daze celebrating my bravery, there was a call for officers to assemble. I headed off to see what our next move would be. I followed the other officers and saw the same weary look on their faces. There was little chatter until Major Shenton started to address the group.

"Gentlemen, I am to pass on congratulations from General Howe for our resounding defeat of the so-called Continental Army." He waited for a response. It didn't appear that anyone felt like celebrating. He continued. "General Washington has done us the great service of opening up the road to the Rebel capital. We are to march into Philadelphia today and capture the city and every Rebel left there."

Captain Taylor spoke up. "Major, do we have time to see to the wounded?"

I noticed Shenton scowling at Taylor. I then noticed the heavy bandage wrapped around the Captain's right arm. Taylor seemed to shrink from the look.

"This should be a time of celebration. We have the opportunity to capture the Rebel capital and end the war. There is no time to waste. Go form up your men. We are to commence the march within the hour. Dismissed!"

I followed the other officers out into the sunlight. I turned to Lieutenant Worthington. "Do you think the war will be over?"

He looked down and shook his head. "I don't believe that Mr. Washington is going to surrender his Army after yesterday, do you?"

We gathered every man that was able to march and started for Philadelphia.

Chapter 24

Anne Smith

A Baby Girl

M y plan to go south and find Peter would have to wait. Our little bundle of joy decided to come into the world a little early. I laid in bed with rivulets of perspiration pouring off my body. I tried to focus on the window in our bedroom between contractions. My world was in the moment between watching billowy clouds pass by and enduring the jolts of evenly spaced cramps. The pain was unbearable, but the midwife remains gentle and patient with me. Both my mother and Amanda were present to help me through the delivery. As I willed my body to push, I heard a squeal as the baby took its first breaths. Then both grandmothers yelled out, "It's a girl!" My mother squeezed my hand and Amanda kissed my forehead. The excitement turned to doubt as I saw the look on the midwife's face. She whispered something about the amount of blood that I was losing. About that time, I remember fading away, barely hearing the voices of the women in the room taking care of me. I felt a longing as my baby was taken into another room before I could see her. Then darkness.

I awoke a few hours later and looked around the bedroom. There was no one else in the room. Maybe I had dreamed it all. Then a wave of pain hit and I cried out. The first face I saw was Amanda. She called over her shoulder, "She's awake." Amanda came and sat next to the bed. "How are you feeling, Anne?"

I focused on her face. "Where is my baby? Is she alive?"

Amanda smiled. "She is wonderful. She has the face of an angel."

I tried to sit up but collapsed. I whispered, "Can I see her?" The next thing I noticed was my mother coming into the room holding a bundle in her arms. "Anne, would you like to meet your daughter?"

I nodded my head. She gently placed the baby on my chest and backed away. I stared down at the sleeping face. I lost control and started sobbing.

"What is wrong?"

I blinked the tears away and choked out an answer, "She looks so much like Peter and he is not here to see her."

Over the next few weeks, I regained my strength and bonded with my baby. Peter and I had long discussions before he left on what names we would use. If it was a girl, we decided she would be called Beatrice after Peter's birth mother. The name seemed to fit. I hoped that she would have a better life than her namesake.

I suffered bouts of melancholy mixed with the joy of being with Beatrice. My mother told me that was normal and I shouldn't be concerned. All I know is that I can't raise our baby by myself. I needed to know how Peter was doing. Beatrice doesn't sleep through the night and constantly wants to feed. My body still hasn't recovered from the birth. I do the best I can.

I sporadically receive Peter's letters, but he paints a picture of safety and dullness. I have my doubts. He still doesn't understand that I need him to be truthful with me at all times. I must stay strong for Beatrice. I still plan on going south when I am able. Maybe I'll go after this winter.

—ℓℓ—

As the weather starts to turn, I still take my daily walks. I push Beatrice in her pram and feel the invigorating rays of the sun on my face. I enjoy this time of year as the leaves start to change colors and there is a chill in the air. It is our special time together away from the annoying interference of the grandmothers.

When I returned home, I'm faced with visitors in my parlor. Both my father and John Smith were there with the grandmothers. Each had a solemn look on their face. I nearly collapsed thinking that something happened to Peter. I tightly grasped Beatrice to my bosom. "What is this about?"

John came to me as Amanda took the baby from my arms. He guided me over to the sofa and sat me down. "There is news."

My eyes welled with tears. I sat up straight. "Tell me."

"There was a great battle in New Jersey. A great many men were killed or wounded."

I leaned toward my father-in-law. "Is Peter....dead?"

John took a deep breath and took my hands in his. "We don't know. My sources only tell me that the Army suffered a defeat and the British captured Philadelphia."

I pulled away from him and leaned over. I covered my face with my hands and lost control. I felt arms holding me as I screamed out. They let me get it out of my system. I sat back up and wiped my face with the hem of my dress. I felt embarrassed to show weakness. After a few minutes, John spoke. "The last letter I received from Peter, he told me that he was given the rank of major and would report to General Greene. We heard that General Greene's men were heavily involved in the fighting. We have to assume that Peter was involved. We just don't know at this time how he is. I'm doing everything I can to find out any news about my son."

I stood up. "Then it's settled. I have to go and find out for myself."

My father stepped forward and for the first time spoke. "Is that a smart thing to do?"

I just glared at him.

"Anne, the weather is turning. Winter is on the way. What about Beatrice?"

"Father, I will take my daughter with me to go find her father."

Two days later, I was on the road in a carriage driven by John.

Chapter 25

Peter Smith

Valley Forge

The men were dejected after the battle. The Army was in shambles and we had surrendered the field to the British. It took time to care for the wounded and resupply. After licking our wounds for a few days, General Washington decided we would make winter camp at Valley Forge. I reminded the men that we had saved the day and prevented the enemy from destroying our Army. We lived to continue the fight with the British, ultimately gaining our independence. My words seemed hollow as we faced another defeat even with a sound plan. How do we get past the poor execution of solid plans? It took its toll and many men deserted, deciding it was better to go home. I have to admit that the thought crossed my mind again, but I couldn't conclude that I had reached that point. That would mean that all the effort and sacrifice would have been for nothing.

It was only a day's march from Philadelphia to Valley Forge. The weather was turning colder. I was concerned about the effect it would have on the men. When we got to our destination, I could see that the location was prime for a defense against any British attempts to attack. We had a clear panoramic view of the valley below where the British Army would have to pass through to reach our stronghold. There was good access to water and plenty of trees to use for the construction of cabins for the men to dwell in. Would enough supplies reach us to adequately provision the men? That proved to be a misguided concern early on as a steady flow of goods reached us. I wondered what role my father played in that. Thinking of him made me focus on home and Anne. The baby must have been born by now. I considered taking leave and going home, but it didn't seem like the right time to leave the men. I went immediately to my cabin and wrote a long letter to Anne. Who knows how long it will take to reach her?

I shared a cabin with three other officers. At night, we would discuss the plight of the Army and our chances of success against the might of the British. I became close to Major Philip Scribner. He hailed from Connecticut and fought in most of the battles waged to this point. One particularly cold evening as I was mesmerized by the flames of the cabin fire and thoughts of home, he turned to me.

"Peter, can I ask you something?"

I blinked at the smoke in my eyes and turned toward him.

"I have only heard tales about the sea battle where you lost your arm." He pointed at my empty sleeve. "Can you tell me what happened?"

I hadn't talked about that day for a long time. I sat quietly for a few minutes. The snores of our two cabin mates could be heard above the crackling of the fire. "It's not anything that I'm proud of." I looked at him and he remained silent. "There were three ships sent to seek out and engage British shipping. We encountered two British Men-of-War and the ship I served on, the Triumph, broke off to engage one of the ships. I was the gunnery officer and I was with the gun crews when the ship came into range." My voice became grave as I recalled the moment. "We fired our guns prematurely, doing little damage to the enemy ship. They unleashed a volley that badly damaged half of my guns. The explosion sent me flying against the bulkhead ruining my arm." I still could feel my missing arm and there was some pain. "We were able to still maneuver and got off a second volley which disabled the British ship. I went to report to the captain when the British started to tie up and board our ship. I reacted out of pure hatred and grabbed a sword and led some men to meet the threat." I could see the surprise in his eyes even in the barely lit room. "I then led the men aboard the British ship and captured the crew."

There was silence for a few moments, other than the crackle of the fire. "Is it true that you killed the British Captain?"

I couldn't bring myself to tell him the whole story and my history with Captain Auger. I shook my head and that was the end of the conversation.

Chapter 26

Nigel Crittenden

Rebel Capitol

W e marched into Philadelphia unopposed. A large contingent of loyal citizens turned out to welcome us. I assumed that all the rebellious crowd had made their escape. We were treated as liberators. It was refreshing to be seen in such a light, and I could see the men's demeanor change. It didn't quite take away the horror of the battle at Brandywine. Still, there was a noticeable skip in their step as they marched down the wide streets of the city. I was impressed by the tidiness and grandeur. It was a smaller version of New York, yet it had its unique personality. These Americans continued to surprise me. Well, they are transplanted Englishmen. I was told that the colony was founded by Quakers and I saw the tall steeples of churches crowding the city center. I wondered about the logic of occupying the rebel capital instead of seeking out and defeating Mr. Washington's Army. I assumed that General Howe knew what he was doing. He was a general and I was a lowly lieutenant. What did I know?

We were placed in Germantown, north of Philadelphia. The officers were billeted in the homes of locals. The house that I was stationed in was the home of a rebel sympathizer. The servants that stayed behind told me that the owners fled when they heard the news of our troops heading this way. They also indicated that the master of the house was known to entertain members of the rebel government. The man was wealthy and the house was well adorned. I questioned the wisdom of backing a failed attempt at revolution over loyalty to the King. I had much to learn about these Americans. One thing was true, their Army fought valiantly.

We were ordered to set up defenses against a possible attack from the Rebel Army. We also sent out patrols daily to keep an eye on the Americans up in those hills outside the city. Other than that, there was little to do. The men became bored and there were incidents of violence against the locals and their property, much like what we saw in New York. It was a challenge to maintain discipline knowing that the men were restless and needed an outlet. Another issue was keeping the army provisioned. As part of the daily patrols, the men were required to locate supplies for the Army. This didn't go over well. It started innocently enough attempting to pay the locals for items needed to feed the Army, ending in outright theft of whatever they could take. This tactic changed many loyal citizens' views of us and our occupation.

While all this went on, the general staff held elaborate parties in the city. These were attended by the wealthiest loyalists and the upper echelon of the Army. Of course, I was never invited. It must have been like the final days of the Roman Empire, where the ruling class celebrated while everyone else suffered. It was going to be a long winter.

In April, General Howe was relieved of command by General Henry Clinton. There was an extravagant party thrown in honor of General Howe. It was a macabre ending to his reign as commanding general. There were rumors that his inaction led to the defeat that General Burgoyne suffered at Saratoga in upstate New York. It was an embarrassment that could not be overlooked by the King and his government. We knew that there would be orders from the new commanding general. It would be good to end this occupation duty and get back to winning the war.

I was summoned to another all-officer meeting with Major Shenton. I followed the other officers in the regiment to the house where the major was quartered. There was much discussion amongst us as to what this was about. I kept my mouth shut and just listened. When we got to the home, we were ushered inside a large study. Major Shenton was leaning over a desk where a large map was laid out. When we all had filed into the room, he looked up.

"Gentlemen, we have received orders from General Clinton's staff that we are to abandon Philadelphia and return to New York." There were audible gasps. Captain Taylor was standing beside the major and spoke out. "That will be enough of that!"

The major didn't seem to notice. "The general is concerned that the Rebel Army will attempt to retake the city and he deems New York to be more strategically important than Philadelphia."

"What about General Washington's Army?"

I turned to see who said that, but could not tell. Major Shenton stood erect and his eyes sent daggers around the room. "We are not to question the orders that we receive. I require each of you to go back to your commands and prepare your men to sail north to New York. You are dismissed."

There was silence as the officers exited the house. I turned to Lieutenant Worthington, "Percy, what do you think it means? We were so sure that we would end the war by capturing Philadelphia and now we go back to New York."

He didn't look at me, but replied out of the corner of his mouth, "The defeat at Saratoga must have been worse than we were told. Maybe we are losing this war."

I felt as though I had been punched in the stomach. That couldn't be true. Would I never get my chance at avenging my father's death? That sent a shiver through my bones. I also couldn't stand the thought of getting back on a ship. On the other hand, we would be going north....closer to Boston.

Chapter 27

Anne Smith

On the Road

We rode in silence for a few hours. I glanced over at my father-in-law, but I couldn't read what he was thinking. I was grateful that he didn't try to talk me out of my quest to find my husband. I had my doubts about dragging a baby along on a trip that could be laced with danger. What sane mother takes their newborn across unfamiliar territory, especially during a revolution. It was chilly in the open carriage and I held Beatrice tightly against my bosom. I bundled her tightly in blankets to protect her from the elements but she was shivering. John saw me clutch my daughter.

"Do we need to stop and find shelter?"

I stared out at the empty countryside. There were only uneven rows of trees that acted as sentinels guarding the isolated road. Where were all the people at? "We should press on, at least until we come to the next town."

He grunted and slapped the reins to get the horse moving at a quicker pace.

After more silence, I asked, "Do you think I am foolish to try and find Peter?"

He snorted. "It's not foolish to want to see your husband to make sure he is unharmed."

"But...."

"Listen, Anne, I think you are the strongest and most intelligent woman that I have ever met. I just would hate for something to happen to you and Beatrice."

"Why did you agree to accompany me?"

"I couldn't let you go by yourself. I also need to make sure my son survived the battle. It would also be prudent for me to see for myself if my efforts to supply the army are working."

"Then it's settled. We will go find Peter."

Over the next two weeks, we slowly made our way through the backcountry trying to avoid New York City. One of the innkeepers in Connecticut warned us that the British Army was in the process of relocating to the city and that we should avoid it at all costs. It could add a week to the trip. I was disappointed about the delay and the missed opportunity to see the city. I heard all kinds of tales about the grand buildings and all the modern wonders that Boston didn't have. Peter mentioned to me about his time in the city. His opinion was quite different, and he preferred Boston. Maybe we could stop there on the way back home.

Most of the small villages we stopped in were friendly and welcoming. We received a lot of questions about traveling with a small child in the winter. We had to be careful about how much we shared about our mission. It was sometimes difficult to gauge the loyalty of the people we ran across. One way or the other. I found it odd that every colonist wasn't taking a united stand against the King.

Once we reached the border between New York and New Jersey, the weather took a turn. We were greeted by the effects of an early spring. The warmer weather was refreshing and gave us hope that we were getting closer to our destination. We were having a grand day and decided to stop early in Germantown for the night. As we entered the town, both of us gasped at the lingering signs of the battle that had taken place. Destroyed buildings lay abandoned at the edge of town and debris was scattered along the way. This put an immediate damper on our improved spirits. It brought back the reality of what we were facing and what could have happened to Peter. As we slowly moved through the center of town, there weren't any signs of either army, just the resulting damage. We stumbled on an inn that was still intact. The name on the outside indicated it was the "Blue Bell Inn." It was a two-story, white-washed dwelling. I carried Beatrice inside while John took care of the carriage and horse. It was cramped but clean inside. I didn't notice other tenants. It would be nice to have our privacy but it was troubled because of the lack of other guests. I walked over to the proprietor. His eyes were riveted on me.

"Sir, I was wondering if you had accommodations available for the night?"

He looked at Beatrice and smiled. "Just one room?"

"No, we need two rooms. My father-in-law is seeing to our horse and carriage."

He had me sign the ledger. "What brings you out this way?"

I took a minute to try to read his intentions. "We are searching for my husband. He's an officer in the Army."

"Which one?"

"Continental."

"Well then, you are certainly welcome here."

I let out a nervous breath. "Do you have any news about where the Army is right now?"

"After the battle, they went into their winter camp at Valley Forge. That's only a few miles from here."

Just then, John came into the inn. "John, good news. The Army is camped near here."

He sat our luggage down and reached out to the innkeeper. "John Smith, pleased to meet you, sir."

The old man took his hand in a warm embrace. "Pleased to have you here, Mr. Smith. My name is Perkins. Let me know if there is anything you need. Dinner will be served in an hour."

"Can I ask you a question, Mr. Perkins?"

The man nodded.

"How bad was the battle?"

"Well, there were two battles. One at Brandywine and the other here in Germantown. They were bloody affairs, but the Continental Army made a strong showing against the redcoats."

I gasped at the mention of a "bloody affair." "Have you heard of my husband, Peter Smith?"

He thought about it for a few seconds. "Can't say that I have, Ma'am."

Chapter 28

Peter Smith

Going South

T he weather slowly started to improve. With the onset of spring, the camp became a quagmire of mud, but it was a welcome reprieve from the bitterly cold weather we endured. The change in seasons also had a positive impact on the morale of the Army. Those men who survived their time at Valley Forge will always have a special bond. As far as I'm concerned, I think this was the turning point for our little army. We had gone through so much disappointment and defeat, but there was a core group that made up what would be considered a professional army instead of a loose group of militias.

Drilling began in earnest as General Washington prepared us for up-coming campaigns to defeat the British. There was also a push to recruit new men to the cause to rebuild those lost souls who chose not to or could not serve anymore. There were rumors abounded that the French would finally come to our aid. There was a sense of hope that we could actually gain our independence. I knew that there were many long days ahead of us, but I joined in the belief that we could gain our freedom.

The constant drilling had a positive effect on the men. We regained that elan that was lost during our winter slumber. My breast would swell with pride as the men were put through their paces. On a particularly warm day, I stood at the head of a column of men marching around the common area, when I looked up on the ridge above and noticed General Washington sitting atop his horse watching our progress. I barely knew the man, but his presence was magical to the Army. I felt the pride a father must have for his son's achievements as there was an added step in the march of the men as they noticed their commanding officer reviewing them.

After the day's drilling was concluded, a staff officer of the general found me. I was sitting outside my cabin when I noticed Lieutenant Colonel Alexander Hamilton walking in my direction. I knew that he was well thought of by General Washington, but I knew very little of the man.

"Major Smith, you are a hard man to find."

"How can I help you, Colonel?"

He stopped and labored to catch his breath. "I came to collect you for a meeting with Generals Washington and Greene."

I stood up abruptly. "Do you know the meaning of the meeting, sir?"

He looked around to see if anyone was listening and leaned toward me. "Very exciting news. You are to be sent to the southern colonies to prepare the defense for a possible British invasion."

I took a step back with the news. Then I remembered that this was the reason I was let back in the Army in the first place. "Lead the way, sir."

He grinned with satisfaction from my response. "Follow me, please. I will accompany you."

He led me to the quaint two-story, brick home that was Washington's headquarters. Two guards were standing at the entrance. They eyed me as I entered. We walked into a spacious room that acted as the general's office. He was seated behind a large desk. There was something awe-inspiring about being in the presence of the larger-than-life man. I never felt at ease around him and my breathing was shallow while waiting for him to notice me standing there. General Greene was across from him and had his back turned toward me. They seemed to be caught up in a serious discussion when Colonel Hamilton announced our presence.

"Sir, I have located Major Smith."

Both generals looked up. "Thank you, Colonel." General Washington turned to me, "Welcome, Major."

I came to attention. "General Washington, General Greene." General Greene nodded his head.

"General Greene has informed me about your leadership under fire during the battle at Brandywine Creek."

I was rather embarrassed and looked down at my boots.

He continued. "I have received intelligence that the British are planning to send troops down to the Carolinas to open another front. General Greene and I would like for you to take five hundred men to Charleston to strengthen the defenses there." He watched for my response.

"It would be my honor, General Washington."

General Greene motioned for me to look at the map that was spread out on the desk. I stepped forward and looked at where he was pointing. Laid out on the map were the positions of both armies.

General Greene spoke up. "We want you to march your men down through this route." He pointed to the roadway he alluded to. "Along the way, try to enlist as many men as you can."

I had a hundred questions running through my mind. "Would it not be more expedient to travel by ship?"

They looked at each other. Washington broke the silence. "Major, we do not have ships available to take you. We also believe that you will have ample time to get to Charleston in time to assist the garrison there."

"Yes, sir."

General Greene interrupted. "Colonel Hamilton will see to your provisions. Select your men and be on the road within a week. We want you to send us timely correspondence about your progress." He then smiled at me. "One more thing, Smith. We feel that for such an undertaking, you should be promoted to Lieutenant Colonel." He came around the table and shook my hand.

"Make us proud, Colonel Smith."

I walked out of that room as if I were walking on air. Stopping abruptly outside the headquarters, I thought about Anne. I had not received a letter from her in weeks. Surely she was busy attending to our child. Then I felt a sudden dread. What if something was wrong? I couldn't shake the unsettling feeling and raced back to my cabin to write a letter telling of my promotion and assignment.

Over the next few days, I worked with my staff to select men to march to South Carolina. We were looking for volunteers and not surprisingly easily reached our quota. I found that Colonel Hamilton was very organized and provided us with most of the supplies that we would need to make the journey. He equipped us with wagons and a herd of cattle to feed the men. He also found a way to provide us with five canons and additional muskets, ammunition and powder. There were even new uniforms for the anticipated recruits that we would enlist. I was amazed at the amount of supplies. He told me that the French were steadily providing us with the materials of war to defeat their hated enemy, the British.

On a hazy, overcast morning in early April, we started on our seven-hundred-mile trek. I rode at the head of the column with my adjutant Captain Miles Hampton. General Greene was present to see us off. As we neared the general, I threw him a salute. As he returned the salute, he called out, "Godspeed, Colonel."

I felt confident that we would accomplish our mission, but I still couldn't shake my doubt about not hearing from Anne.

Chapter 29

Nigel Crittenden

Back to New York

I finally made peace with getting back on another transport ship. It was no wonder we couldn't defeat an amateur army when our generals couldn't find a consistent plan to execute. As we prepared to march back to the piers in Philadelphia, word came down from General Clinton that we would march back to New York City instead of sailing there. There hadn't been an explanation, but the rumors were rampant that the French had entered the war on the side of the Americans. I asked the other officers to see what they had heard. I only received blank looks in return. A large French fleet was reported to be in the area and there must have been concern about losing several troop transports. So we'll march.

After spending months in winter quarters, it was a relief to finally leave Philadelphia. The men were in good spirits as we headed north through the countryside of New Jersey. I admired the lovely scenery of open fields surrounded by thick stands of forests made up of hardwood trees. There was an abundance of wildlife to subsist on. I thought again about the possibility of settling here after the war ended. It was so different from England. There was so much land for the taking. A man could make something of himself in the colonies. Still, I was troubled by the news of the French. It could make the task of defeating the Americans much more difficult.

The important question to me was where is Peter Smith? There was a lingering thought in the back of my mind that gnawed at me. It had something to do with that American officer I saw at Brandywine. I couldn't put my finger on it. I would eventually figure it out. Going back to New York would be closer to Boston, but how would I get there to look for him? There could be no rest for me until I laid that scoundrel in the ground.

It took a few days to reach the outskirts of New York City. It was depressing to be back in another city that we had already captured. It was as if my life was on a never-ending repeat cycle. This time, there was little fanfare from the citizens on our return. They did not look happy to see us. I felt the same about them. We camped at the north end of Manhattan awaiting orders. There were scattered discussions in the ranks about the odd ways of the officers. I snorted when one of the men told his companions that it would make more sense to just defeat Washington's Army where they were and then hang the man for his treasonous acts against the King. That summed up how I felt about our predicament. If a common enlisted man could see the simplicity of the strategy, then why couldn't the generals?

We stayed camped in those fields for weeks waiting for the generals to decide what to do with us. It was more monotony for the men to endure. We tried to keep them occupied, even letting them have passes to the city to provide them with a diversion. Nothing seemed to work. While we stayed in camp, recruits from England filtered in to replace the losses we sustained. From their appearance, I assumed that the prisons back home had been emptied to supply the Army. There was also an effort to enlist local Tories to come to our aid to fight for our mutual cause. This had little success and the men that joined were unreliable.

As summer turned into fall, we had little to do other than participate in scrounging expeditions into the countryside of New York. Our orders were to scout for any Rebel units in the area, and more importantly to locate supplies to feed the Army. This was the low point of my time in America. There were days when I seriously considered taking my leave and heading to Boston to conclude my unfinished business. I supposed that all the lessons that were drilled into me in military school prevented that from happening. Even as I considered how I would find and dispatch Smith to avenge my father, I couldn't abandon my duty. This would have been an affront to everything I believed in.

Chapter 30

Anne Smith

Continue the Journey

My eyes bolted open to the cries of Beatrice. She must have slept through the night because I finally got a good night's rest. I stretched and flung my legs over the side of the bed and sat for a few seconds trying to collect my thoughts. I got up to comfort her. The time I spent with my daughter was the best part of my day. I held her close while she fed on my breast. It suddenly dawned on me, today might be the day that we get to see Peter. Beatrice seemed to feel my nervous energy and she started to babble. There was a quiet rap on the door and John poked his head in.

"I wanted to check on how you're doing."

I covered my exposed breasts. "We are well. Do you think that we will find Peter today?"

He averted his eyes. "I was thinking the same thing when I woke up. I will go downstairs to arrange for breakfast so that we can get an early start." He closed the door and I burped Beatrice. I dressed both of us and headed downstairs.

We got directions from Mr. Perkins to the encampment at Valley Forge. We rode through the countryside and giddily discussed the possibility of finally catching up with Peter. The excitement I felt made me forget any doubts that I had that something terrible happened to my husband. Perkins told us that it could take a couple of hours to reach the camp, so we continued to chat and enjoy the scenery.

At last, we came to an opening in the trees. My jaw became unhinged. What I saw shocked me to my bones. There were rows of shabby-looking cabins surrounded by groups of men who were dressed in rags. I turned to John. "Surely, this can't be the Army?"

He sat up on the edge of the carriage bench and scanned the camp. He took off his hat and shook his head. "We had reports about the poor shape the men were in, but I never expected this."

We continued down the muddy road until we were stopped by two armed sentries. "Hold up there!" The men stepped in front of our carriage and one of the men grabbed the reins of the horse. The other soldier walked around us looking in the carriage. "What is your business here?"

John held out his hands. "We are here trying to find my son, Peter Smith."

The soldier looked at me and Beatrice. "Who might the lady be?"

"I am Peter's wife and this is his daughter."

The sentry smiled. "Not sure who Peter Smith is."

John proudly announced, "He is a major of a contingent of men from Massachusetts."

"Is that so? We'll see about that." He turned to the other sentry, "Johnson, escort our guests to headquarters to see if anyone knows this Major Smith."

We slowly followed the soldier as he trudged through the deep quagmire of a path. As we neared the center of the camp, we got a better look at the horrible conditions. It was appalling what these men had to endure staying at this place. I could only imagine the suffering that went on. We caught the attention of a number of the men and they gathered around us curious to see a woman and a baby. My heart went out to each of them.

The soldier led us to a house that was surrounded by soldiers. He started talking to what appeared to be an officer and pointed at us. The officer nodded his head and came in our direction. He tipped his hat. "Private Johnson indicated that you are looking for Major Smith?"

"Yes, sir. We have not heard from him and I wanted him to meet his daughter." I held Beatrice up so that he could see her. He smiled and seemed to consider what I said.

"If you would follow me, I'll take you to Colonel Hamilton. Maybe he can answer your questions."

The young man assisted me to climb down from the carriage. We followed him into the house. The soldiers guarding the entrance eyed us suspiciously. We were led to a room in the back of the house. "Wait here while I speak to the Colonel." The officer disappeared into a room and we could hear them talk about us. We were then directed to enter the office. Colonel Hamilton came from behind a desk and introduced himself to us.

"I am Colonel Hamilton, the adjutant to General Washington. I understand that you are looking for Major Smith."

His tone was carefree and joyous. I was hopeful for answers. "Yes, sir. He is my husband. This is his father John Smith."

He bowed at us. "Please have a seat." He turned toward John. "Are you the same John Smith who is responsible for supplying the Army?"

John looked uneasy. "Yes, sir."

"Well, then I must commend you on your efforts that likely saved the army over the winter."

I looked at John who let out a breath of air and sat back in his chair. Colonel Hamilton then turned toward me. "Mrs. Smith, your husband is a true patriot and was instrumental in preventing the British from annihilating our Army. He was promoted by General Washington to Lieutenant Colonel for his bravery and leadership."

As Beatrice squirmed in my arms, I responded, "That is wonderful, sir. Can we see him?"

He placed both hands, palms down, on his desk and tilted his head. When he finally looked back at me, there was sorrow on his face. "You just missed him. He was given orders from General Washington to go south. He left only two weeks ago."

The joy of knowing that he was still alive was replaced by the shock that we were too late to see him. Tears welled up in my eyes and I sat back clutching my baby.

The Colonel stood up and handed me a handkerchief to wipe my eyes. "I'm so sorry that you missed him. I can only say that the orders he received were vital to the success of our cause."

I wiped my eyes and composed myself. "Are you able to tell us where he went? We would like to continue our journey to find him."

I watched him closely as he folded his hands as if in prayer and thought about my request. "It could be dangerous for you and your baby to follow him." He must have read my mind from the glare I threw at him. "It is nearly noon. Please let me discuss this with General Washington. I will have someone see to your needs while you wait."

We were led to another room that had a wash basin. Beatrice continued to be fussy. She must be hungry. I asked John to leave so that I could feed her. I was so disappointed about the news that I felt helpless. I blamed God for this injustice. We were so close to reuniting only to be teased with success. I knew that no matter what I had to continue looking for him. There was a knock at the door.

"Anne, can I come in?"

I covered up. "You can come in."

John opened the door and made sure it was safe to enter. "We have been invited to have lunch with General Washington. Colonel Hamilton didn't give me any indication if they would share Peter's mission with us."

We were led to the dining room. The smell of cooked meat and freshly baked bread was overpowering. Before we were seated, a tall man entered the room. He had a quiet air of authority. I determined this must be George Washington.

He bowed at us. "Welcome, Mr. Smith, Mrs. Smith. Please join us for lunch."

I was intimidated by being in his presence. He was cordial and kind. A gentleman's gentleman. The meal was wonderful. I hadn't tasted anything this good since we left Boston. There was small talk going on around the table. Apparently, John knew the General. He never told me about that. I ate in silence. I was about to burst waiting for the right time to ask about Peter. Finally, the General put down his fork and glanced my way. "Mrs. Smith, I have given much thought to your predicament." He paused. "Against my better judgment, I will allow you to continue your search for your husband. While I can't tell you exactly where he is being sent, I will provide you with an escort to get you safely to him."

I maintained my exposure while thinking to myself, *I don't need your permission.* "Thank you, kind sir."

He nodded. "It's the least I can do to reunite your little family for all that your husband has sacrificed." He seemed to be pleased with himself, but I could detect sadness in the man. The responsibilities that he carried had to be daunting. "All that I ask is that you stay the night and get some rest. You can get an early start in the morning."

"I would be agreeable to that."

After a sleepless night, we were provided with some provisions and an escort of six mounted soldiers. As promised, we got an early start. I tried to start a conversation with one of the men to gain information about our destination. The man politely refused to answer my questions. So we continued our journey. Hopefully, we will find Peter before something else happens.

Chapter 31

Peter Smith

Loyalist Militia

We slowly wound our way through the forests and hills of southern Pennsylvania. I had nearly five hundred men under my command. Along with the men, we had wagons and a herd of cattle. The caravan was spread out over a mile. I was advised that there shouldn't be any British troops in the area, but I was warned about bands of Loyalists who could create problems for us. We made steady progress until we reached Brandywine Creek. It was surreal being back at this place. It didn't help that there was a blanket of fog covering the river. It made me think back to that fateful day when we were flanked by the British and nearly destroyed. This was the first battlefield that I had visited after the battle. I looked over the ground and replayed the fighting in my mind. I concluded that we did all that we could on that fateful day. I scanned the faces of the men. Many of them looked around as if searching for ghosts or possibly redcoats.

The spring runoffs from the surrounding mountains made the creek almost impassable. We had to take time to erect a bridge large enough to accommodate the wagons. It cost us a day's delay. During the crossing, I stood on the banks and watched in horror as one of the wagons threw a wheel and the driver couldn't control his spooked team of oxen. Both he and the wagon went off the bridge. I stood helpless as the man was dragged downstream. His screams could be heard above the din of the roaring river. Death on the battlefield I understood, but when it came to avoidable accidents it was hard to take.

We pressed on. I hadn't been given a specific deadline as to when we should reach Charleston. The intelligence only indicated that the British planned to try and capture the city. I had to also fulfill the other part of my mission to recruit along the way. To achieve that purpose, I sent some officers ahead to the small villages that were on our path to hang notices and speak with the locals.

Our efforts at recruiting showed inconsistent results. When we entered the city of Lancaster, there was a crowd of over a hundred people who welcomed us as conquering heroes. We signed up twenty men to a one-year enlistment. Then we entered the sprawling city of Baltimore in Maryland, where we were jeered and asked to leave. Obviously, we did not sign up any men. However, we did receive a warning about a band of Maryland Loyalists commanded by Colonel Chalmers. The man who provided the information was of dubious character and stated that Chalmers had a thousand men at his command. I had my doubts but sent out scouts in all directions to ascertain their location.

We were averaging ten to twelve hours a day on the road. I had little time to think of anything but getting safely to Charleston. When I let my mind drift, I thought of Anne and our child. I wondered how old the baby would be right now. Before leaving Valley Forge, I wrote a long letter to Anne and my parents. There was no guarantee as to when, or if, they would receive the correspondence. I couldn't dwell on that right now.

We continued at a steady pace, trying to hug the coastline as much as possible. There were inherent complications of crossing rivers and dealing with impassable swamps. We neared the border with Virginia when one of my scouts came riding up to me. I watched his face for any indication of the news he would present. His eyes were wide with fear. I braced myself.

"Colonel, I have spotted that Loyalist group. They are up ahead in that dense thicket of trees." He pointed excitedly.

I followed his arm and saw the road bend into a section of forest. "What numbers are we facing?"

"I counted about a hundred men, all on horseback."

"Very well, Private." I turned to my aide Captain Charles Wentworth. "Captain, spread the word. Get the men lined up to prepare for an attack." He saluted and rode back to the column. I watched as the men orderly spread out across the road in columns of two. I ordered that a detachment be sent back to the wagons to guard them and the cattle in case this was just a ruse.

The line of men moved forward. I followed behind them on my horse to get a better view. The ranks started to get broken up by the mass of trees. Then I heard the unmistakable sound of sporadic gunfire. There was a roar from my men as they returned the fire. As smoke rose from the battle, I was unable to make out any details. I rode closer and was surprised by the buzzing sound of a musket ball that barely missed me. As the sound of gunfire erupted, my head swiveled to the rear. The wagon train! I wasn't sure if I should stay put or ride back to check.

For a few minutes, the balance of the battle seemed to change hands. Then the sound of gunfire started to abate. I could see Captain Wentworth riding back to give me an update.

"Colonel, we have them on the run. They put up a good fight. We were too much for them."

"What about casualties?"

He took off his hat and wiped his brow. "No exact count yet. There are several men who received wounds. Not sure about the dead."

"There was an attack on the wagon train. Go back and check on the status." As the Captain rode off, I wondered how this would affect our progress.

I was stunned by the numbers. We had suffered fifteen killed and forty-five wounded in the skirmish. The enemy had fared much worse. We killed thirty-five and captured fifty, most of them wounded. The Loyalists were able to capture one of the wagons and made off with some of the cattle. All in all, it was a successful fight. Against my better judgment, we set up camp to attend to the wounded and get some rest. We stayed in camp for three days. I had no idea what to do with the captured Loyalists. I couldn't bring them with us and I wouldn't bring myself to execute them, so I paroled them and made them promise to go home and not fight anymore.

Off to Virginia. Hopefully, they will be more receptive to us.

Chapter 32

Anne Smith

Heading South

It was good to be back on the road. I still had mixed emotions. On one hand, I was grateful that Peter had survived the engagement at Brandywine. On the other hand, I still couldn't come to grips that we had just missed seeing him. It's as if he was beyond my stretched-out fingertips. We had been apart so long that I started to forget what his face looked like. My dreams were filled with premonitions of doom. Why had my father's God forsaken me?

Our escorts were polite and attentive to Beatrice and my needs, but they stayed tight-lipped about our destination. Who would I tell if I knew? The scenery remained the same, thick forests dotted with tiny villages. It all became a hindrance rather than something to enjoy. We are such a small party that we did not receive much attention. The few people that we met along the road asked us where we were heading. I didn't know how to answer them. I had a strong urge to ask them if they saw Peter's regiment pass this way, but my escorts gave me knowing looks.

I became concerned about the toll that this was taking on John. I knew that he wanted to see Peter as much as I did, but the separation from Amanda was hard on him. He wouldn't admit it to me, but the physical impact on his health had to be difficult. He must have known that I was thinking about him, as he turned my way and gave me a subtle smile.

"How is baby Beatrice?"

I was holding her tightly while she slept. "I believe that she is enjoying this adventure. It's a shame that she will not remember any of it."

He leaned closer to me. "I have been questioning our guards and they won't give up any information." He threw a thumb over his shoulder. "Back at the dinner with General Washington, I heard some officers talking about some concerns about the Carolinas. If you have been paying attention, we have been going south. My guess is that is where Peter is being sent."

I sat up higher in my seat and swiveled my head around. "How can you tell?"

He chuckled and kept his eyes on the road. "Keep an eye on where the sun is. We are also getting closer to the coast. I would guess that we are going to either Charleston or Savannah."

I couldn't control the surprised look on my face. "How can you possibly know that?"

I asked much too loudly.

He admonished me with his eyes. "With my work to supply the Army, I know that there are garrisons at each city to prevent the British from capturing those strategic places. Our cause could be dashed if the enemy could establish themselves in the southern colonies."

I held Beatrice tighter against me, almost waking her. "What does this mean for Peter?"

He shrugged his shoulders. "It could mean that he will be in harm's way again."

We continued the rest of the day traveling in silence.

Chapter 33

Peter Smith

Mount Vernon

After the recent skirmish, I was more mindful of our security. As a precaution, I sent out scouts to ensure that there wouldn't be a repeat of the attack in Maryland. Maybe I was paranoid from the incident with the two drunks on the road and the latest assault by the Tory militia. Was I being tested by a higher power for my stubbornness? No matter what, our mission was the most important thing and we continued to look for recruits. We needed to grow the ranks and replace our losses. The farther south we went, we found the men of the villages we passed through to be more receptive to join us. I was surprised because the struggle had mostly been in the northern colonies. At least that's what I thought.

The day we came to the Potomac River was magical for me. From a commanding river bank, I scanned across to Virginia. The sight was breathtaking. Spread out in front of me was a vast land filled with flowing rivers and dotted with grand plantations. This is where General Washington's home was. The General had shared with me his love for his home and talked longingly of the fertile land that grew an abundance of crops. He asked that we stop at Mount Vernon and check on his wife Martha. I hired a local man to lead us through southern Maryland to our destination. The

Potomac was more imposing than I anticipated. I could not see any bridges and turned to our guide, Mr. Mitchell.

"Mr. Mitchell, where is the best place to cross?"

He pointed to the grand home of General Washington atop a hill. "To the south of the plantation, the river goes around a slow bend. The water in that area is usually not as deep. Your men should be able to cross safely."

I looked to where he pointed. From this vantage point, the river looked imposing and not passable. I had my doubts. "Please lead the way, sir."

He led us down a winding path that paralleled the river. I shook my head as I scanned the breadth of the rushing waters. Up ahead the river disappeared around a sharp curve. I followed the old man and true to his word, the river was calmer and looked to be passable. He turned and smiled at me.

"Colonel, if you can get someone to cross over and tie a rope to one of the trees on the other side, then your men can use the line as they cross."

I turned to my adjutant, Captain Hampton. "Captain, see to it."

I sat on my horse and watched in silent amazement as the men slowly crossed the river using the rope. There were some issues with a few men slipping on the bottom of the river bed and losing their grip on the rope. It only proved to be a minor embarrassment for the drenched soldiers. Everyone made it across.

It took more than three hours to complete the transit. I thanked Mr. Mitchell and headed for the palatial home of George Washington. Riding up to the house, I couldn't help but notice the slaves working in the fields. There must have been hundreds of them. They looked as amazed to see us and I was them. Against the yells of their white overseers, they stopped what they were doing and watched us march past. I was still appalled at the practice of indentured servitude. Back when I was a child on the ship, I heard tales from the other sailors about slave traders transporting men, women and children from Africa to the New World. I thought that it was just fairy tales; like mermaids and sea monsters. Unable to do anything about it, I turned my attention to checking on Mrs. Washington.

She was standing on the front porch awaiting our arrival. I knew that she had been in the camp at Valley Forge, but I had not met her. She was petite but stunning. Her dark hair had started to gray and she wore a pleasant smile. I dismounted and walked up to her. Her eyes rolled from my face to the empty left sleeve. I removed my hat and bowed.

"Welcome, Colonel. My husband sent word that you would be stopping by."

"Yes, Ma'am. He asked that I check on you."

She led me into the house. "As you can see, I'm doing well."

I looked around the finely appointed house. There was a beehive of activity as the servants were attending to the running of the mansion. She pointed to a seat in the front parlor. It was a large room, two stories high and ornately furnished. There was great wealth in this place. She poured me a cup of coffee and sat across from me.

"How long do you and your men intend to stay, Colonel Smith?"

I took a sip and set the cup down. "No more than a day or two. We have experienced some delays and need to make up some time."

"Am I allowed to ask where you are going?"

I sat back in my chair and considered the question. Considering that this is the wife of the commanding general, "We are to march to Charleston to aid in the defense of the city against a proposed British invasion."

She nodded her head. She must have already known. "You are welcome to stay as long as you need. I have already made arrangements for an area to camp your men. I have also told the kitchen to prepare a meal."

I stood. "Thank you Ma'am for your hospitality."

We stayed for two days at the plantation. It was the longest we could afford to stay. I didn't want to insult our host by leaving too early. She would invite me to have lunch with her each day, but I declined begging forgiveness for duties that I needed to attend to. Truthfully, I was intimidated by her. She was much more refined and intelligent than I was.

The morning we left, it was raining and the dirt roads had turned into a mucky mess. I didn't want to second guess my decision to leave and we made the best of it. It rained for three solid days and we continued to hug the coastline of Virginia. The weather caused delays. We had to halt the column often to push wagons and cannons out of the thick mud that clung to everything. The men started to show signs of weariness, yet we pressed on. On the fourth day, the rain let up and the humidity was oppressive. Most of the men hailed from the north and hadn't experienced this type of torture. This was closely followed by an assault from small flying insects that were intent on sucking all our blood. This incited another round of complaints. A soldier's prerogative.

After a short night's rest, we entered the port town of Yorktown. I had been warned that there were several Tories in the city and the British Navy ported ships there regularly. I decided to play it safe and camp on the outskirts of the city. I did send some of my men to check on the reports of British ships and to get a sense of the loyalty of the citizens. The men reported back a few hours later stating that there were no British to be seen and they received a frosty reception from the locals.

We left the next morning.

Chapter 34

Anne Smith

Good News

I was mindful to watch the position of the sun everyday to confirm what John told me. We were indeed going steadily south. Our small band of travelers continued to draw little attention from the locals. We made good time, but I doubted we were catching up with Peter. It had been a tiresome journey and I was concerned about the impact the long days on the road were having on Beatrice. Was I a terrible mother for bringing her? I couldn't have brought myself to be without her and I wanted her to meet her father.

We were delayed crossing the Potomac River until our escorts could find a path across. After crossing at a shallow bend in the river, one of the escorts mentioned to me that he was from Virginia and pointed out the Mount Vernon plantation. His name is Reynolds and he talked in reverence about General Washington and his wife Martha. My curiosity was piqued. "Do you think it would be possible to call on Mrs. Washington?"

He looked at the other men around him and stood up in his saddle to get a better look at the large house on the hill across from us. "I will ride ahead and see if it would be proper to visit unannounced."

I watched with anticipation as he rode off even though this would delay us catching up with Peter. I was excited to meet the famous woman. It was a pleasant day and I welcomed the warmer weather. John was playing with Beatrice and seemed to be immune to what was going on around him. After a few minutes, I could see Captain Reynolds riding back at a gallop.

"Mrs. Smith, Mrs. Washington has graciously agreed to a visit. I explained who you were and the purpose of the visit. She seemed to be excited to share some news with you."

I reached over and squeezed John's shoulder. "Do you know what she is talking about?" John looked up to see who I was talking to.

Captain Reynolds chuckled. "No, ma'am. She did not share that information with me."

We traveled up the path that led to the majestic home. I began to take notice of all the slaves working in the fields. It wasn't the first time I had seen slaves. There were some freedmen in Boston and there was a scattering of them along our trip. Nothing could have prepared me for the volume of human bondage that I was witnessing. It took some of the excitement away from meeting Martha Washington.

As we rode up to the entrance of the plantation house, Martha came out to greet us. She was smartly dressed in a long dress. She smiled broadly and walked up to my side of the carriage. "Mrs. Smith, it is a pleasure to meet you."

I stepped off the carriage and she gave me an unexpected hug. I blushed at the attention. "Mrs. Washington, this is my father-in-law John Smith and my daughter Beatrice." John held up the baby so that she could see her.

"You must be tired from your journey. Please come in and have some refreshments. We have much to discuss." She led us into her home. My excitement was about to overcome me with her tone and demeanor. We sat around a small table and coffee and sandwiches were delivered.

"Captain Reynolds told me about the purpose of your trip. I have some very good news about your husband." She paused for effect. I wanted to jump out of my seat.

"You just missed him. He was here about two weeks ago checking on me as a favor to my husband."

I could barely contain my emotions. "How is he doing? I have not seen him since before Beatrice was born."

She patiently nodded her head. "He is doing well. He has no idea that you are looking for him, I assume."

"I sent letters, but I don't believe he knows."

"Do you know where he is going?"

"No. Our escort hasn't told us anything."

Martha looked around to ensure that none of the escorts could hear her. "Your husband and his men are being sent to Charleston to reinforce the garrison against a possible British invasion."

I thought to myself, so John was correct. I sat up straight. "Thank you for sharing that information."

"My pleasure, dear. You should know."

I looked over at John. "We should be leaving." He nodded and started to get up.

"Are you sure? You are welcome to stay with me to get some rest from the road."

I reached out and touched her arm. "Thank you for your hospitality, Mrs. Washington. I am anxious to catch up with my husband. I'm sure you understand."

She stood and nodded. "You are a brave woman, Mrs. Smith. I know a little about having a soldier for a husband. I wish you safe travels and good luck."

We were back on the road and I turned to my father-in-law. "You did know where Peter was going." He only smiled and continued to hold the reins. I'm not sure that I felt any better about the situation knowing where Peter was being sent. I did know that I had to reach him before the British did.

Chapter 35

Peter Smith

Charleston

We spent the next two weeks trudging through southern Virginia, North Carolina and into South Carolina. There were an endless number of rivers to cross and swamps to avoid. Continuing on our mission to recruit, we stopped often trying to grow our ranks. I began to see a pattern of pockets of Tories and Patriots. There were horrible tales of retribution played out by both sides. It was personal with the settling of old grudges instead of acting out of loyalty to a side. Still, we were able to recruit dozens of new men. This replaced our losses and allowed us to increase our strength. How well these men would fight when the time came was still to be seen. The closer we got to Charleston, the better I felt about our prospects to defend the city. It wasn't clear the number of troops already stationed there. I had been briefed about a prior attempt by the British to capture the city. That was back in 1776 and the city's defenders held off the invasion. Surely the defenses had been strengthened to prevent another attempt.

We entered the grand southern city on a late summer day. We marched proudly into the outer defenses manned by our fellow patriot soldiers. They were excited to see us and came out of their trenches to cheer. I didn't get any indication that they were expecting us. There was no sense of danger. These men had no idea what they were about to face. That's if Washington's spies were correct.

I was escorted to the headquarters of General Robert Howe while my men were being billeted. I had never met the general before and knew very little about him. I studied the line of defenses laid out while riding to see the general. There didn't seem to be any concern on the soldiers faces and there was little discipline. How well would these men fight when the time came?

I entered the gates of Fort Moultrie and into the presence of General Howe. He stood to greet me and I saluted him. He had a puzzled look on his face. "Colonel, what is the meaning of this?"

I stepped forward and handed him my orders. He stepped back and began to read the document. "I see General Washington believes that the British are returning. As I'm sure you saw, there has been little to be concerned about since their first failed attempt."

The man was very conceited and I instantly did not care for his demeanor. "General, the commanding general has intercepted correspondence indicating that the British will be making another attempt to capture Charleston and possibly Savannah."

He slumped back down into his chair. "We have not heard from the garrison at Savannah in a while. I decided that there was nothing for them to report." He sat quietly. "How many men have you brought with you?"

"Sir, we have almost seven hundred men," I said proudly.

"I should tell you, Colonel, that I am to be replaced by General Benjamin Lincoln. I have been ordered to take command of the forces at Savannah.

I will place you and your man on the outer defenses for the city. General Lincoln can do with you what he pleases after he gets here."

I watched the faces of the general's staff as I saluted and left. He certainly doesn't inspire much confidence. Maybe General Lincoln will take this more seriously.

We settled in and began to train the recruits. The other officers watched with interest. I utilized the "Regulations for the Order and Discipline of the Troops of the United States" which was written by General Friedrich Wilhelm Steuben. I had the distinct pleasure of meeting the profane man from Prussia. He was a Godsend when the army was at its lowest during the stay at Valley Forge. I swore by the manual's teachings. I believed that this convinced the other officers to adopt the standards and start drilling their soldiers.

I felt better about our chances after a few weeks of preparations. At night, I wandered around the city. Its beautiful row houses along the battery were stunning. I was fascinated by the vibrant pastel colors splashed on the mansions. They were unique and filled with opulence. The wealth in this area was unlike anything back in Boston. I had to remind myself that this wealth was on the backs of the slaves that made many of these men rich beyond belief.

I gradually acclimated to the heat and humidity. There was always a pleasant breeze off the harbor to cool it down to a tolerable level. It was by standing on the sea wall that protected the city, where I would look out at the defenses around the harbor. Charleston was a peninsula like Boston. It jutted out into the harbor and was surrounded by two rivers that flowed from the interior into the harbor. It seemed that the fortresses were capable of covering all the entrances where the British would sail their fleet. What if they decided to take a less direct route and attack from the land side?

It's times like these when I think about Anne the most. If she has written, none of her letters have reached me. I continue to write to her, but I can't tell her where I am. After all this time, I struggled to reveal my feelings to her, or anyone. I have been through so much in my young life, yet I have always felt inadequate and not deserving of love. I pursed my lips at the thought of how Anne has accepted me for who I am and given me unconditional love. Am I a fool to have left her to run some ridiculous errands while I have already given so much to my country? Every time I started to have these doubts, I thought back on my life in England and how the British had treated me and my adopted country. Then I understand why I made the choices I had.

I stood at the sea wall staring out at the harbor when it all became clear to me. We will never win our independence if we always wait for the British to make the first move. At some point, we needed to take the battle to them. While I had the utmost respect for General Washington, I had to question his handling of the war. We should fight on the offensive and drive the redcoats from our lands. I'm resigned to the fact that this is where I'm supposed to be and I needed to make the best of it. Time to get some sleep.

Chapter 36

Anne Smith

Reunion

Being on the road for this long was taking its toll on Beatrice, John and me. John didn't look well and he desperately missed Amanda. My buttocks were constantly numb from sitting on a wooden bench and bouncing over uneven roads. Poor baby Beatrice had to endure hours of the bumpy ride while trying to sleep or feed. On other occasions, there was a rhythm to the movement of the carriage. Like the gentle sway of tree branches from an unseen breeze. As it would rock back and forth, I would escape into myself and picture what life would be like after all this. I smiled thinking about being in our large home back in Boston filled with children and having their father home every night.

Captain Reynolds indicated that we should reach the outskirts of Charleston today. It all seemed so surreal and I was too tired to be excited. I looked up at the cloudless sky. It was going to be another scorching day. I longed for the cooler weather back in Boston. I couldn't understand why anyone would want to live in this area. The heat and humidity were oppressive and all the varieties of insects constantly attacked us. I had to remind myself why I was putting us through all this. It was about seeing and supporting my husband.

When we reached the edge of the city, I could see the tall spires of the churches and the sails of ships in the harbor. Even John seemed to perk up with our destination in view. Our small escorts looked with amazement at the surroundings. I clutched Beatrice and whispered in her ear. "You shall see your daddy today."

We were stopped at a checkpoint on the main road leading into the city. Two bored-looking soldiers questioned Captain Reynolds. I couldn't hear what they were saying, but the Captain pointed at me and the guard shook his head as if he understood. Reynolds rode back to us.

"Mrs. Smith, the guard told me that your husband is stationed at Fort Moultrie out on the peninsula." He pointed in the direction where the fort lay. They are providing us with a guide to take us there.

"Thank you, Captain. Can you believe that we finally made it?"

He smiled and led the way. I turned to John and squeezed his arm. "Thank you for helping me find Peter."

"It will be good to see him." He smiled weakly.

We had to backtrack to get to Sullivan's Island where the fort was. We are so close now and my anticipation was building. It took the better part of two hours to reach the fort. From my vantage point, it didn't look very imposing. As we neared the structure, we got the attention of the soldiers there. They must not receive many guests. Captain Reynolds rode ahead. I watched as he questioned one of the soldiers, who pointed toward some buildings ahead. I stretched my neck to get a better view. John pointed the carriage in that direction.

To my great joy, I saw my husband come out of one of the structures. He was looking straight ahead to see what all the commotion was. I saw the moment that he understood who we were and he ran in our direction. I shouted, "Stop the carriage," and jumped down while clutching my daughter in my arms. My focus was only on Peter. We were the only people in the world. He reached me and held me at arm's length. "Anne, is it you?" His face was glowing with pure pleasure.

I held Beatrice out in my arms. "Peter, I want you to meet your daughter, Beatrice."

His face was in shock as he beheld his daughter for the first time. I handed her to him and he held her in his arm and couldn't take his eyes off her.

"This is such a wonderful surprise. How did you know where to find me?"

Just then, a voice interrupted us. "Son, it is so good to see you."

Peter looked over my shoulder and saw his father. "Father, you came to see me."

"I came to make sure that your wife and daughter got here safely."

"How is mother?"

John broke his eye contact and mumbled, "Her health is poor and I need to get back to her."

I could see that this was overwhelming to Peter. He tried to take it all in and then said, "You must be exhausted. Please come into my quarters and I will get you something to eat." He barked out some orders to take care of the carriage and horse. I saw a tear in his eye when he turned toward Captain Reynolds. "Thank you, Captain, for bringing my family to me."

That night when everything calmed down and Beatrice was fast asleep, we had our first moments alone. We had been apart for so long that it was awkward at first. Then desire took over and we passionately embraced and a demon overcame Peter as lust took over. It was rough and animated love making. When it was over, Peter had a hard time making eye contact with me. He whispered. "I'm so sorry. I'm not sure what came over me."

I held him tightly. "It will be better next time. Go to sleep."

We settled in over the next few days. Peter found suitable housing for us nearby and we were finally a happy little family. It warmed my heart how he interacted with Beatrice. I could tell that he was elated to be a father. He indicated to me that this post was not what he anticipated when General Washington assigned him here. It was a tedious duty for a man who wanted to be in the middle of the action. It was a Godsend to me. He was safe away from all the fighting.

My father-in-law booked passage on a ship heading to Boston as soon as he could. The travel had taken a toll on him, but his concern over my mother-in-law overrode any concerns he had about his health. We stood on the pier in silence for a few minutes, until John turned and with his voice cracking, "It's time for me to go home. I shall miss all of you dearly. I will make sure to give mother a hug from each of you."

I handed Beatrice over to him for one last snuggle. "Thank you again for seeing me safely to Peter." He pursed his lips together and handed the baby back. I had an unsettling feeling that it would be the last time I would see him alive. When I scanned his face, I believe that he had the same feeling. Peter was speechless and looked to be oblivious to any bad omens, but he had a troubled look about his father leaving so soon. We watched the stooped over, elder Smith walk up the plank and take his place on deck with the other travelers. It was interesting to watch the ship's crew undo the heavy lines holding the ship to the pier and set the sails to leave the harbor. We stood there until the ship sailed out of sight.

Chapter 37

Peter Smith

Goodbyes

I couldn't express the joy that I felt when I saw Anne and Beatrice. I couldn't believe my eyes. It was like seeing a mirage and not comprehending its meaning. There had been no indication that they were following me to South Carolina. Of course, I would have forbade her to come here not knowing how dangerous it may be. I struggled with her possibly being in danger from the immanent British attack, even while enjoying the company of my small family. Beatrice was everything that I dreamed of. The sight of her smile melted my heart. The distraction of having them here is powerful and made me question why I stayed at this tedious post.

Our first night together was a nightmare. I'm ashamed at losing control and taking my wife as one would a harlot. Something overcame me and I was only thinking about myself. I knew that I hurt her both physically and mentally. I tried to apologize for my actions, but she just dismissed it. We never spoke of it again.

It was difficult for me to say goodbye to my father. It was bittersweet for me to escort him to the ship that would carry him back to Boston. It was like reliving my first trip there. Standing on the pier watching him climb aboard the ship and breathing in salt air, took me to that dark place where the British ship had been my personal hell. I secretly wondered if this would be the last time that I would see the man that had given me so much. These weren't the distractions that I counted on when I agreed to come here.

It was a hot and humid summer mixed in with torrential downpours that caused flooding to this low lying area. There haven't been any updated reports of British activity in the area. Maybe Washington was wrong. We continued to build up our defenses in preparation for a British invasion that had yet to materialize. This kept the men occupied, but garrison duty could be tedious. Most of these Yankees had never been this far south and I was concerned about them missing their families and deserting. Unlike our time spent at Valley Forge, we were well supplied here. The surrounding plantations provided a steady flow of provisions. This went a long way in maintaining good morale.

The summer passed quickly as we waited for any sign of the British. It gave me time to spend with Anne and Beatrice. We settled into the home that we were provided and our evening walks around the island gave us time to thank our blessings. We took advantage of these moments to talk about our future. I considered this to be one of the happiest times of my life. I brought up the possibility of staying here after the war. She seemed to have reservations, but did not discount the idea outright. Anne took to her role as an officer's wife and she acted as a surrogate mother to some of the younger soldiers. Beatrice was walking and babbling constantly. This gave her mother and father hours of entertainment. It was a good life. How long would it last?

As the weather started to cool with the change of seasons, there were troubling reports that the British were at last making a move in our direction. These reports were received by headquarters in Charleston, but were weeks late. It was the belief from General Lincoln that the attack was imminent. We were ordered to prepare for an assault from the harbor. This caused a dilemma for me. What do I do about Anne and Beatrice? I had made acquaintances with some of the surrounding plantation owners. These families were strident supporters of our cause and I was certain that one of them would take my family in during the crisis.

The Boone family was one of the families willing to take Anne and Beatrice in. The Boone Hall plantation was located about ten miles from Fort Moultrie and more importantly far enough away from Charleston that I felt my family would be safe. I took time from my busy schedule to take Anne and Beatrice there myself. The entrance to the grand plantation was surrounded by huge oak trees covered in moss. It was an odd sight seeing the clumps of stringy moss hanging from the branches. I had never seen anything like it. The view down the dirt path surrounded by the large oaks to the mansion was breathtaking and added to the grandeur of the place. Even little Beatrice looked amazed at the sight. The residence was larger than any other I had ever seen. It was a two-story, red brick dwelling with four large chimneys. The entrance was adorned by four huge white columns that only added to the opulence. As we rode up to the elegant home, we saw a large number of slaves working around the house and surrounding fields. Anne and I discussed this dilemma on multiple occasions. We were both repulsed by the practice, but we needed the assistance of these people if we were ever going to win our independence. We agreed to be polite to our hosts and not bring up the subject. It was like giving up a little bit of my soul.

We were met at the entrance of the grand plantation house by the current owners, Mary and Joshua Toomer. Mary was the granddaughter of the original owner. They seemed to be excited to see us and as Mary fussed over Beatrice and Anne, I walked off with Joshua. "Joshua, I appreciate you looking after my family."

He tilted his head. "It is my pleasure, Colonel Smith. Do you have any updated news about the British arrival?"

I kicked at some rocks in the dirt road and slowly shook my head. "I fear that we are receiving news from General Washington weeks after he sends it. We can't be sure if they will be here tomorrow or in a month." I stopped and turned toward him. "We appreciate everything you have done for the Army." I hesitated trying to keep my composure. "This is the most important thing that I can ever ask you. Please keep my family safe."

He looked taken aback by my show of emotion. "I will personally make it my mission to see that no harm comes to them."

We returned back to the carriage and I said my goodbyes. As I drove away from the plantation, I couldn't bring myself to look back. It seemed like I was always deserting my family.

Chapter 38

Nigel Crittenden

Savannah

J ust as the air started to turn noticeably colder announcing the change of seasons, we received our next set of orders. I had assumed that we would spend another winter camp here without facing the American Army again. I had considered taking my leave and going north to Boston. I learned that it was only two hundred miles away. While I sat idle for weeks, I seriously considered going. It's too late now. The orders were certainly welcomed, but somewhat surprising. We were to reboard transport ships to sail from New York to the colony of Georgia. There we were to be part of an effort to capture the prize city of Savannah. It was explained to us that this would be an important mission to isolate the southern colonies and require Mr. Washington to break up his army in response. It was welcome news going to a warmer climate. I wondered what became of the French fleet that kept us bottled up in New York. Did they just disappear?

A week later, we boarded the transports and made our way out from New York into open water. I stayed on deck to watch the city disappear. I wondered if I would ever return. Good riddance, I did't have pleasant memories of the city or its people. The sea was rough and the ship rocked with the assault from each wave. My stomach rebelled with each unwelcome movement. I watched as the other officers who had put on brave faces trying to endure the elements started vomiting their breakfasts onto the wooden deck. I was able to keep my decorum and my meal. Maybe there was a little bit of my father in me. I was fascinated by the precision of the ship's crew. They acted in sync to control the ship by handling lines and sails in a choreographed manner. Each man fulfilled a specific duty. It was a precision that my father must have appreciated. I imagined that this was why he loved to be at sea.

After nearly a month at sea, we were alerted to the sighting of land off the coast of Georgia. I raced up to see for myself. It was a welcome sight and my pulse quickened with anticipation. We were promised warmer weather in the south, but there was a chill in the late December air. We were offloaded a few miles south of Savannah. As soon as the roughly 3,500 troops under the command of Lieutenant Colonel Archibald Campbell were organized, we began our march to take the city. We had not been provided with any information about the strength of the defenders. At least we were taking the offensive. It was exhilarating that a commanding officer was making the decision to go right into battle instead of scouting the position for weeks. Now that I had a taste of battle, I would be better prepared for what was to come.

We made our way through swampy ground that slowed up our advance. There was a stench that was overpowering as we waded through the murky knee-deep water. After clearing the marshy terrain on the outskirts of Savannah, we could see the defense that was established on the hills surrounding the city. This could be another bloodbath as the rebels held the high ground and had an open field of fire. I squinted to get a better look at the entrenched enemy it didn't appear they were manned by many rebels. Did they not know we were coming? I couldn't believe our good fortune. We were ordered to spread out to outflank the thinly manned lines. As soon as we were in position, the order came to move forward. I braced myself for the unmistakable sound of gunfire. As we advanced within a few hundred yards, the shooting started. I tensed, but the random shots were few and off-target. I held my sword out in front of me and continued to lead my men. When we reached the American lines, the enemy hastily retreated. This was nothing like Brandywine.

I quickly made an accounting and we had not suffered any casualties. We caught our breath and waited for more orders. I noticed Captain Taylor making his way in my direction. I went to meet him. He smiled and said, "Crittenden, we have them right where we want them. They have all retreated into the city. Our scouts reported that there aren't more than five hundred men aligned against us." He turned and scanned the field ahead of us. "We have information from an African slave that we can take an unguarded route through the swamp to avoid the enemies' lines." He pointed to the man. "I want you to follow that man and take the city."

I turned to see what man he was pointing to and noticed the darkest man I had ever seen. He was scantily clothed and looked around at the red-cladded Army surrounding him with some fear. I turned back to Taylor. "It shall be done." I turned to Sergeant Clarke. "Clarke, collect the men and follow me." I went to the slave. "I have been told that you are to lead us around the American Army." He averted his eyes but nodded his head. I would think about the man's lot in life later. I had other more pressing matters. He took off and I followed. I didn't turn to see if my men we were following me.

The man led us to the right of the American defenses. We were under cover from the trees in the swampy area. As we came into the open, I could hear the opening volleys from both sides to our left. I looked around and there wasn't a rebel in sight. I directed the men to work our way back to the left to attack the flank of the American line. It was a total surprise when we assaulted their exposed line. The Americans began to flee in terror as we reigned fire down on them. We wadded through their wounded and dead capturing the men who hadn't the strength to flee. Just as quickly as it started it was over. We had captured the important southern city of Savannah.

Chapter 39

Peter Smith

Bad Intelligence

While we focused on an impending invasion of Charleston, we received word that the British captured Savannah. This was a crippling development. All the British had to do was march inland to take Charleston from land instead of by sea. I was called to headquarters to meet with General Lincoln and his staff. There were signs of panic among the locals as I rode over to Charleston. I wondered to myself, how could we have missed that? I believed that General Washington's spies would have warned us.

I reached headquarters at the same time as many of the senior staff. I could see the general as he paced nervously around the room. General Benjamin Lincoln was an older man. He was pudgy and looked to be in ill health. He was from Massachusetts and made his name during the victory over the British at Saratoga. I made my way through the throng of officers. Lincoln stopped, looked up and nodded at me. "Gentlemen, we have received word that the British have overwhelmed and captured the troops defending Savannah."

I looked at the stunned faces of the other men standing around the general. Even though there was a chill in the room, I could feel the thick tension in the air.

"That means that the British now control all of Georgia. They will likely target Charleston next as a design to control South Carolina. This could have dire consequences for our interests in the South."

There was only silence.

"We must remain diligent and redouble our efforts to save the city. Each of you return to your commands and see to the construction of stronger defenses. I expect the British to take us both by sea and land. It may be too late, but I'll see what I can do about getting reinforcements."

"What about the French?"

I turned to see which officer said that. I was thinking the same thing.

Lincoln shook his head. "It doesn't appear that we can count on the French helping us at this time."

My mind raced as I rode back to my command. I questioned the logic of trying to defend this entire area with only 6,000 troops. Surely the British would bring more men to bear along with their fleet of ships. I didn't question the orders I've been given, but wouldn't it be better to preemptively attack the redcoats on the ground of our choosing? Only time would tell. At least I was able to get Anne and Beatrice away from this place.

Chapter 40

Nigel Crittenden

Occupation Duty

There was much discussion among the officers about the ease with which we captured Savannah. The Rebels had to know how important the city was to protect the Southern interior. We now had access to the Savannah River from which we could capture all of Georgia and South Carolina. It should also make it easier to capture Charleston from land, instead of a direct landing against the strong defenses on the coast. For now, we celebrated our lopsided victory. Each victory against the rag-tag Continental Army made the possibility of losing the war unthinkable.

We were ordered to perform occupation duty. This was an all too common task. I was quartered in the home of a Loyalist family along with other officers from the regiment. The family was very gracious and took good care of us. It was much preferred over camping in a tent. It was interesting how the Loyalists came out in droves after we had run off all the Rebels. It appeared that we were destined for the monotony of another winter camp. At least the weather here was more agreeable. I would lead small parties in the surrounding area to scout for any of the enemy that stayed behind. It was pointless duty. We never found anyone within miles who would admit to being a supporter of the rebel cause.

As the winter months dragged on, there was little to do. I began to take daily walks through the city. It was lovely. It was laid out in squares with an abundance of parks surrounded by elaborate homes. There was one thing that I detested and that was the institution of slavery that was ingrained into Southern society. I toured the massive plantations that grew tobacco and rice and was deplored by the state of the slaves. They were treated poorly and made to live in shacks. It was ghastly and not Christian behavior. When I spoke with the plantation owners and other wealthy men in town, they all stressed the importance of the slave trade to their very likelihood. I remained polite and tried not to be judgmental in their presence out of respect for their loyalty to the King. Still, it bothered me that they prospered on the backs of others who had no say. I equated it to the Americans continuing to talk about how they had no say in the way they were governed. Ironic stance to take. I was aware of the history that the British Empire played in the slave trade. Hadn't we disavowed the institution?

Another issue that remained on my mind was finding Peter Smith. I have been in America for nearly two years and I was no closer to finding him. I don't know if it is fate that kept us apart, or if I needed to prove myself in battle before I'm allowed to seek my revenge. It's an intriguing dilemma that I faced. The way the war was progressing seemed to indicate that we would defeat the Americans in short order. Then what? Do I stay here to find him on my own? Maybe he had already been killed. I certainly hoped not. I wanted to look into his eyes when he died so I could remind him what he cost me and my mother.

Nothing more I could do now, just continue to do my duty to King and country.

Chapter 41

Anne Smith

Plantation Life

Just when I got used to being reunited with Peter, he sent us out in the middle of nowhere. Boone Hall was majestic and our accommodations were exceptional. Still, I would rather be by my husband's side. I have been assigned a slave by the name of Sally. She is a pleasant-looking young woman with sad eyes. She was always in a good mood around me and I wondered if it was forced. She looked after my every need. I had never been taken care of in my life like this. I struggled with someone "serving" me. When Mary Toomer was not around, I tried to make conversation with Sally. I could tell by the look in her eyes that there was danger in her being anything more than my maid. I would never understand why these Southerners think that it's proper to own other human beings. There was even an older slave named Betsy who looked after Beatrice. I hoped this arrangement wouldn't last very long. Peter couldn't answer my repeated questions about how long until we reunited in Charleston.

There was little for me to do to occupy my time. I wasn't allowed to help out in the kitchen or any other household duty. It made me feel useless. So I would take daily walks around the plantation. I learned that the two main crops grown were rice and indigo. I was fascinated watching the slaves standing stooped over in knee-deep water working to cultivate the rice. It had to be back-breaking labor. I absently wiped the sweat from my brow. How do they work every day in these elements? I could tell that I made the overseers uncomfortable when I walked around unescorted. They didn't mistreat the slaves while I was around. I wasn't naive and it made me wonder how they were treated when I wasn't near.

As hard as I tried to strike up conversations with these poor people, the more they resisted. I could only assume that they had been warned not to talk to me. That didn't stop the children from flocking to me when I was near. They seemed oblivious to their surroundings. It was the only life they had ever known. So I guessed it wouldn't be a surprise that they wouldn't question the way they lived. I even tried to sneak into one of the pitiful cabins where they resided. I was politely escorted away. Why has God forsaken them?

For dinners, I was expected to dress up. Since I didn't bring anything remotely passable with me, I was provided with suitable clothes. These meals were filled with awkward social rituals that I was not trained in. Mary would guide me through the niceties of the affairs, but I struggled to adapt. As women, we were treated like second-class citizens and not allowed to express our opinions on topics that I was interested in, like the war for independence or politics. We were expected to run the household, raise children and look pretty. This was something that I worked my entire life to change back home. These debutantes didn't seem to look at women's rights the way I did.

I was thankful that Peter was more open-minded about my place in the world. I missed him dearly.

Chapter 42

Nigel Crittenden

Transfer Request

As the days turned into weeks, I was tired of garrison duty in Savannah. Other than leading raiding parties into the countryside, there was nothing to do. I was spinning my wheels in this place, getting no closer to helping defeat the rebels or finding Peter Smith. I considered relinquishing my commission and going to find Smith on my own. This was an all too common reaction that I had to my circumstances. At my lowest points, I even considered going back to England and taking care of my mother. After months of not hearing from her, I was pleasantly surprised when a packet of letters arrived from her. I slowly made my way through her correspondence. She longed to see me and expressed her concerns for my safety. She also reluctantly spelled out the health issues that she was facing. The overriding theme of her letters was requesting the status of my finding and killing Peter Smith. She seemed to emphasize this above all other things. She made it clear to me that it was my duty to avenge her husband, my father.

I faced a conundrum. Do I continue to do my duty or go after Smith? I decided on another option. I went to my commanding officer to ask for a transfer. As I walked toward the house where Major Shenton was billeted,

I practiced what I would say. The closer I got the more doubts I had about this strategy and sweat was rolling down my back. The thick summer air was choking my throat. I pulled at my collar and reluctantly trudged on.

I was about to turn around when I heard, "Lieutenant Crittenden, good to see you. Are you looking for someone?"

I twisted my neck and saw Captain Taylor ambling toward me. I thought to myself, what do I do now? I came to attention. "Captain Taylor."

The pudgy man was out of breath. He was also dripping sweat from the humidity. "What brings you to headquarters?"

My mind raced for an answer. "I was hoping to speak with the Major, sir."

He eyed me suspiciously. "Very well. I believe he is available." He turned back toward the narrow two-story house and led the way. I followed. Well, I'm committed now. We walked up the steps to the front door. My stomach was rolling and my pulse increased enough to make me lightheaded. Entering the parlor, I could see the Major sitting at his desk sipping on a cup of tea.

He looked up. "Crittenden, what brings you here?"

I looked uneasily from Taylor back to Shenton. I cleared my throat. "Major, I was hoping to discuss the matter of a transfer with you." I watched his face twist into unbelief.

"Why, pray tell, would you want to do that?"

I didn't envision this going this way. "Sir, I believe that my energies could be put to better use than garrison duty." My voice was higher pitched than I intended.

Shenton sat back in his chair and rubbed his chin. "Did you hear that, Captain? The young Lieutenant thinks his "energies" are useful elsewhere." Captain Taylor grinned. "Where did you have in mind, young man?"

"I would like to return to New York with the main body of the Army. It is there that the war shall be won and I want to be involved."

He stared right through me processing my request. "So you don't believe that our efforts here in the Southern colonies will assist in winning the war?"

His tone was demeaning and my nostrils flared with anger. "No sir, I don't believe sitting in this godforsaken city is getting us one step closer to winning the war."

"You should watch your insolent tone, Crittenden." He continued to glare at me. I stood my ground. "Put it in writing and I will present your request to the General. Be cautious of what you ask for. Dismissed."

I stumbled down the steps and felt the urge to vomit. As I put distance from headquarters, I realized that I didn't make any friends today. Maybe I should have told him the truth. That might have gone over more successfully.

Time to put my request in writing.

Chapter 43

Peter Smith

Waiting

I pushed the men past their breaking point preparing the defenses. We were isolated and vulnerable to an attack from land. This fort had repelled the first British invasion and I knew that they learned from that experience. As the war drug on, the British seemed to be less sure of themselves and started to take our little army of farmers more seriously. They showed that in their capture of Savannah. They took an indirect route instead of a frontal assault that would have been costly. I wondered if this was an overall strategy to shift the war to the Southern colonies away from the stalemate that was taking place up north.

The work went into the night. It reminded me of that fateful time preparing the defenses on Breed's Hill. I paused to reflect on that tragedy. It seems like it was ages ago and all that effort was for naught. I couldn't allow that to happen again. I requested more munitions so we would be ready for whatever the redcoats threw at us. As the sun's early rays started to come up over the glistening waters of the harbor, it reflected a bright yellow over the ripples. I inspected the earthworks to look for any weaknesses. Speaking comforting words to the exhausted men who lined the wall, I felt a surge of hope. A shout behind me caught my attention and I swiveled my head to see a line of wagons filled with supplies heading our way. The men stood and cheered at the sight. The sergeants started barking orders to unload the powder and ammunition, along with enough food to sustain us through a long siege. Hopefully.

We continued to keep a sharp eye on both the harbor and the narrow entrance to the fort from the land. There was only silence from headquarters. No updates from our spies to the exact date of the invasion. As fall turned into winter, the men started to get restless and there were rumblings. I did the best I could to keep up their spirits while maintaining readiness for anything that could happen. I was never one to throw around corporal punishment, but in times like these, I had to control the discipline of the men under my command. I struggled to make them understand the importance of our mission. There were a few instances where I had to resort to using the whip to make them understand that. I knew that the cabin boy in me was aghast at me for resorting to that form of punishment.

During the lull in the action, I took a trip to see Anne and Beatrice to spend Christmas with them. I understood how this looked to the men, so I devised a plan to let a few men go on leave while making sure that we had enough soldiers left to cover the fort if the British decided to show up. I was so blessed to have my family close, but I still worried about their safety. As I rode toward Boone Hall, I was lost in my thoughts. I was still amazed at how my life had turned out. I could still smell the stench of the streets back in Portsmouth. My nostrils flared from the memory. Then I pictured the face of my mother the last time I saw her. There was a deep piercing pain in my chest. What would she think if she could see me now? I never got to tell her goodbye. Then a different kind of pain emanated throughout my body as I thought about my experience on the Progress. The flood of emotions moved to the exhilaration that I felt when I ran that sword through Captain Auger. Then my thoughts turned to the second chance I was given when the Smiths took me in and raised me to be the man I am today.

I turned the horse off the dirt road that led to Boone Hill. The sight of the tree-lined path that led to the grand house never ceased to amaze me. I wondered what it would be like to have this much wealth. Then my desires were tempered when I started to see the slaves going about their work fueling that wealth. Those poor souls paid little attention to me as I rode up to the house. I had not sent word ahead of my visit and I caught everyone off guard. I smiled as the house servants scurried to find Anne. Then I heard a loud squeal, "Peter, what are you doing here?"

I climbed down from the horse and went to her. I grasped her and tightly pulled her to me. The embrace and kiss were magical and it was as if we were the only people left on earth. I held her at my right arm's length and saw the tears flowing. Her eyes pleaded for an explanation. "Are you here to stay?" I looked away from her gaze. "I couldn't bear to be away from you and Beatrice." I looked around to see any signs of my daughter.

"She is taking a nap." As I was about to say something, I saw one of the house servants, named Sarah, carrying my precious little girl. Beatrice was rubbing her eyes and when she saw me, she let out a yelp. She put out her arms reaching to me. I ran over and scooped her up in my arm. She squeezed tightly around my neck. "Dada." It had only been a few weeks since I saw her last, but she had grown so much. I looked at Anne, who was beaming.

"She is now taking steps and talking up a storm."

We headed for the front door. "You must tell me everything."

That night, our hosts served us a magnificent meal. After dinner, Joshua Toomer and I retreated to the library. He offered me a cigar and a snifter of cognac. Still sore from my ride, I took a seat on a sofa that must have been imported from England. We carried them in our import business back in Boston. They were expensive. Joshua sat across from me and fiddled with his cigar. I knew what he wanted to ask me.

"Colonel, is there any news about the British?"

I sat back and carefully thought about my response. "There hasn't been any word about an imminent invasion. The British usually go into their winter camps, so I don't believe they will strike until spring."

He looked instantly relieved. "You can appreciate that my position supporting the revolution hasn't been good for business. There are many Tories in South Carolina. These people are making it difficult for those of us loyal to the cause to sell our crops. There has been a rash of old scores being settled between the two factions resulting in many deaths. I can imagine that it will only get worse if the British Army gets a foothold in the state."

I heard rumors of such atrocities going on, but it still surprised me. "I assure you we are doing everything we can to make sure that doesn't happen."

He stared at me for more and pursed his lips together. "We shall see."

I stayed until after Christmas. Beatrice was two years old and it was the first Christmas that I spent with her. It was a joyous occasion but muted by the thought of me returning to Charlestown and whatever lied ahead. My focus drifted away from my family back to the business at hand. Sometimes the responsibilities that I carried were crushing. There was no one to blame other than me. I asked for this.

The goodbye was bittersweet. Anne tried to remain strong but broke down. Little Beatrice couldn't understand what was happening. She wailed at the sight of her mother crying. I wiped my eyes as I mounted the horse. There were no words spoken as I pulled at my jacket to protect myself from the chill in the air and turned the horse away.

Chapter 44

Nigel Crittenden

Judas

I submitted my request in writing and after waiting an uncomfortable three days, I was summoned to headquarters. Once there, I was made to wait for over an hour to see Major Shenton. I sat and fidgeted with my uniform, trying to look nonchalant. I watched with great interest as the door to the major's office opened and out stepped General Prevost and his staff. The general eyed me on his way past. I wondered what that was about.

"Crittenden, get in here!"

I stood to face my judgment. I stood at attention in front of the major's desk. He was shuffling papers, then looked up at me with contempt on his face. "It seems that the commanding general has seen fit to approve your transfer request." He waited for a response from me, but I just nodded my head. "I would have thought that you would be pleased."

"I just want to be posted where I can make a difference, sir."

"Then it wouldn't have anything to do with this rebel officer Peter Smith?"

I felt like I had just been assaulted. "How did you find out about that?"

"That is not a concern for you. Lieutenant, this war was not made for you to pursue your vendettas." He slammed his hand on his desk. I jumped back a step. "Do you have any idea where this Smith person is?"

"No, sir. The last I heard, he was in the Boston area. I know that he lost an arm in the fighting and he might not even be in the American Navy anymore."

He rubbed the palm of his hand and tossed the paper toward me. I picked it up and started to read. It was an order to join the fortress at Saint Lucia in the Caribbean. My jaw dropped. I looked up to see that the major was grinning. "What is the meaning of this?"

He was taking great pleasure in my agony. "You requested to be sent where the action is. It appears that the French are trying to capture our territories in the Caribbean. They need experienced officers to defend our interests. You are to report today to the British warship Hermes where you will sail to Saint Lucia."

I was dejected and turned to take my leave without responding.

I walked the city blocks back to gather my belongings. How did this all go so wrong? For a minute I had the strong urge to get on a horse and ride north. It was tempting, but then I would be a wanted man who deserted his post. I could never return to England if I did that.

When I got back to the house I was staying in, Percy Worthington was waiting in the room we shared. "How did it go, Nigel?"

I tried to ignore him, my Judas.

He continued to prod. "Where are they sending you?"

I put down the clothes that I was packing to turn and face him. "Why did you betray me?"

He started to fidget. "I didn't mean to. Major Shenton questioned me about you." He stopped and bowed his head. I waited for more. "He wanted to know why you were requesting a transfer. I thought I was helping you by telling him about Smith."

I started to pack again. "Well, that didn't work. They are sending me to the Caribbean. About as far away as I can be from that man."

I finished packing and headed off to the pier where the ship waited for me.

The transit to the West Indies was fraught with despair. I gripped the rail tightly fighting the urge to be sick. The sea was unusually violent and I could not find my "sea legs." The seawater came barreling over the rails and made it perilous. A sailor saw my despair and told me that we were passing through a monster storm that happens in these waters during this time of year. I hadn't had this reaction before. My father would have been disappointed with me. For the life of me, I couldn't understand his love of the sea. Between bouts of vomiting, I tried to remain on the weather deck as much as possible to get fresh air. The holds below held the worst stenches imaginable. I wasn't the only one affected. There was a line of miserable soldiers who routinely lined the rails.

Pulling into St. Lucia was a godsend. I swore each time I got off a ship that I would never get back on. My opinion changed when I got a good look at my destination. This place was a tropical paradise. It was early winter but the mild temperatures and lush vegetation were intoxicating. The water was a turquoise hue of blue and was clear enough to see all manner of sea life. We had yet to spot any French ships. I wondered if I had been sent on a fool's errand. We were assigned to replenish the garrison defending the island. It was explained to us that the French had unsuccessfully tried to take the island as part of their grand scheme to capture all the islands in the West Indies. The area was strategic for the raw material that they provided, and it was in England's best interest to maintain control of the region.

We disembarked the ship and I had trouble with my balance. Being on a ship for days, my body got adjusted to the constant rocking motion and suddenly there is no motion on dry land. It took me a few moments to orient myself. I could see the smirks on the faces of the other officers as they passed me. We were directed up the north side of the island up to Fort Charlotte. It was a strenuous hike to reach the fort. I bent over to catch my breath and when I stood up there was a stunning sight of the surroundings. I had an unobstructed view of the small island and the other islands surrounding it, especially the island of Martinique where the French had a strong presence. I got a good look at the fortress which had a few buildings and a stone wall lined with cannons. As the men were shown to their billets, I walked over to a British officer who stood stoically watching us. He was a major and looked to be older with a deeply lined face, and steely colored eyes.

I came to attention and saluted. "Major, Lieutenant Crittenden reporting for duty."

He tilted his head while looking out at the small contingent of my men. "Is this all they are sending us?"

I swiveled my head toward his gaze. "There are other reinforcements, but they are being sent to other forts around the area."

He raised his eyebrows and crossed his arms. "The French tried to take this island with a veiled attempt. We were able to keep them at bay, but I doubt a strong concerted effort could be repelled by such a small force."

The man's despair was contagious and a dread came over me. I should have stayed in Savannah. "What are your orders, sir?"

He let out a breath and pointed to a large man who wore sergeant's stripes. "Sergeant Shipley will show you and your men to your quarters. Keep vigilant, young man. We can be attacked at any time."

I walked toward Shipley to see our accommodations. Peter Smith was the furthest thing from my mind.

Chapter 45

Anne Smith

Secrets

After Peter was out of sight, the tears I tried to hold back came flooding down my face. Beatrice screamed in my arms and Sarah took her from me. I sensed someone standing behind me. I turned to see the concerned face of Mary Toomer as she quietly stared at me. I was embarrassed and tried to wipe away the tears with the hem of my dress. Mary came to me and laid a hand on my shoulder.

"Did you tell him?"

I nearly collapsed and she caught me. "I couldn't bring myself to tell him."

She had such caring eyes and continued to hold me. "I'm surprised that he couldn't tell. You are showing."

I stood and turned away from her. "I did everything I could to keep it hidden."

Mary's voice was gentle and soothing. "It is such a wonderful thing. Why wouldn't you share the news of another baby with your husband?"

I hung my head. "He has too much to be concerned about right now and I didn't want to burden him."

"Aren't you concerned that he will be upset when he finds out?"

"It's a chance I'm willing to take. I wish this terrible war would end and we could go on with our lives."

I continued to take a walk every day to clear my head. The winter had settled in and I was surprised how cold it could get here. There wasn't as much activity on the plantation and I tried to speak with the field hands. They continued to shun me for fear of any reprisals they could receive. I was grateful for my hosts, the Toomers, but I felt so alone. The baby was growing quickly and I could no longer hide the fact that I was pregnant. Peter was so close yet so far. I still couldn't bring myself to tell him yet. I hadn't even written to my parents to give them the news.

I rounded the bend through the trees to go down to the marshes where the rice was grown and boats came up the river to take the harvested crops to market. Movement out of the corner of my eye caught my attention. I spied a figure lurking behind an old oak. I swiveled my head to see if I was being followed. My internal alarm was going off and I considered turning around. Something told me to see who it was. I took another quick look behind me and then crept toward the figure. It was a young slave girl. She was scantily clad and was shivering. She had beautiful ebony skin and had to be in her early teens. Her eyes shifted from side to side, betraying the fear she was feeling. I knelt to where she was hiding.

"What's your name?"

She seemed hesitant to talk. "They call me Bitsy."

"Bitsy, why are you out here by yourself?"

"You dat lady at the house with the little girl."

The tone of her voice told me that she didn't trust me. I took her hands in mine. She tried to pull back, but I held it firmly without saying anything.

We sat there for a few minutes in silence and she began to sob. I put my arms around her and started to rock. She stopped crying.

"You can tell me what's wrong. I won't tell anyone."

"How can I trust you?"

"I'm not from here. Where I come from, there aren't any slaves."

She sat up and tilted her head. "Why are you here?"

"My husband is in the Army trying to protect us from the British."

I watched as she processed what I told her.

"Can you take me with you when you go back home?"

My heart sank and I didn't know what to say. "You still haven't told me why you are hiding."

She swiped at her tears. "Massa Richards is looking for me."

I knew that Richards was one of the overseers on the plantation. He was a disagreeable man. I stayed clear of him. "Why is he looking for you?"

Her body shook. "He does things to me and I don't like it."

I sat back and accidentally hit my head on a branch. I knew exactly what she meant. I rubbed my head. What should I do? "Do you come here often...to hide?"

"No ma'am. I usually can't get away. I fear he will beat me."

"I should talk to Mrs. Toomer. She will know what to do."

There was terror in her eyes. "You can never tell her. She will not help me."

Surely no Christian woman would allow this to happen. "Let me try to help you."

She nodded her head.

"Will it be safe for you to go back to your...home?"

"It should be safe after a while."

I reluctantly left Bitsy and went back to the main house. I found Mary in the kitchen. She was supervising the preparation of that night's meal.

She saw me and started to smile, then stopped when she saw my face. "Are you well, Anne?"

"Can I talk to you?"

She led me into the parlor and we took a seat. "I came across one of the field girls named Bitsy during my walk."

Mary squinted her eyes and pursed her lips, but listened.

"She told me a disturbing story about being abused by one of your hired hands."

She didn't react. Her eyes told me to continue.

"The poor child was scared to death about what would happen to her. Is there anything that can be done to protect her?"

I watched her sit back and take a breath through her nostrils. There was danger here.

"Anne, I know that you are not from here and don't understand our ways. I know that these things go on and there isn't anything that I can do about it."

"Couldn't you talk to Joshua about it?" I pleaded.

"No, I will not trouble him with it. We must not ever speak of this again."

A few days later, I overheard the house servants say that the body of young Bitsy was found floating in the marsh where I talked to her. I needed to leave this unholy place.

Chapter 46

Nigel Crittenden

A Familiar Destination

I stood on top of the parapet staring out across the sea searching for the phantom French invasion fleet. There has to be a reason why I was sent here. I put a foot up on the wall and rest my elbow on my knee. Winter in this paradise is an ideal time of year. The temperatures are agreeable, and other than a steady deluge of daily rain, it's perfect. The days pass scanning the sea for any indication of a French armada attempting to dislodge us from our perch. I have to admit that there were a few times that it appeared to be happening. We witnessed a few ships sail between our little island and Martinique and the alarm was raised. Tense minutes were spent waiting for the invasion we all expected, then the ships would sail harmlessly out to open waters. Then it was back to the normal, tedious routine.

At the end of the year, a large number of French frigates came within cannon range and unleashed an ear-splitting volley at our defenses. This was the long-awaited invasion. It was pandemonium as the shells landed among us and we returned fire. The explosions sent up chunks of rocks and debris and I ducked behind the stone wall to be spared. I barked out orders at the top of my lungs to be heard over the striking of the French shells. The men responded with gusto and worked their guns indifferent to the world crashing down around them. Then as quickly as it started, the French sailed off to the north. Other than a couple of lucky hits, we escaped unscathed. Only a few soldiers were killed in the attack and I could not see any sign of damage to any French vessel. It was very odd.

We went through the motions to rebuild the damage done by the French and got back to keeping watch. I resumed my spot on the wall when I witnessed an amazing sight. Over the horizon came a large number of sails. I rubbed my eyes thinking it was an illusion. At first, I thought it was the French returning to finish their attack. I tensed up and prepared to order the men to their stations. Something told me to wait and the closer they came I could see that the dozen or so ships flew the Union Jack. My shoulders instantly slumped. The sense of relief was enormous. The men around me started to cheer. We had gone through a full range of emotions, but why were the ships landing here? I watched with fascination as two of the ships anchored in the bay and sent long boats toward shore. From my vantage point, the men that disembarked from those boats looked like ants. There was much speculation among the men as to the meaning of this new development. It didn't take long for those ants to reach our little fortress. The landing party was made up of several senior officers. I drifted over to hear whatever news they had for us.

Standing in the middle of the pack was an elaborately dressed Colonel. He was tall, rail thin and statuesque. He scanned the fort with an assessing eye and rocked his head up and down.

"Gentlemen, my name is Gerald Abernathy. I have been sent here by order of General Clinton to collect you and your men." He paused and looked around at the group. I scanned the faces of my fellow officers and saw they were hanging on every word from the Colonel.

"You are to take part in the invasion and capture of Charleston."

I stood there soaking in the news. While the Colonel was peppered with questions, my thoughts drifted to the oddity of my time in the Americas. I wasn't sure if this was a sign that I would meet up with Peter Smith or it was just another attempt by God or the universe to make my life complicated. Either way, it mattered little. Orders were orders.

We were ordered to collect our men and possessions and take the long walk down the heights to be loaded on the ships in the harbor. Careful to not trip on my way down the perilous path, I thought about this recent change in orders. I never understood the plotting of the Generals. Why was so much time spent moving us around instead of defeating the Americans in one place? I took a quick look back at the fort that had been my home. I enjoyed being stationed here and dreaded getting back on a ship again.

Once we sailed out of the relatively smooth waters of the Caribbean, the Atlantic gave us a different reception. It was cold and the waves threw our transport around like a doll. My seasickness was worse than ever. At times I prayed for an instant death. God had other designs for me and I suffered along with my fellow soldiers.

Just when it seemed that we would never reach the coast of South Carolina, there was a call from one of the sailors, "Land ho!" I drug my weak and battered body up to see it for myself. Escaping from the stench of the hold below decks up to the weather deck was refreshing. I gulped in deep breaths of air and gazed at the sight of land on the horizon. Then something caught my attention and I swiveled my head to the right. There had to be more than one hundred ships surrounding us. My jaw hung open and I turned my attention back to the coast. There certainly wasn't going to be any surprise to the rebels what our intentions were. I stood there on deck and watched as our warships entered Charleston harbor. It took a few hours, but once in place, they started a barrage on the city's defenses.

It would be a siege.

Chapter 47

Peter Smith

Invasion

I sat in my office reviewing documents when I heard shouts outside. As I stood up the door flung open. I saw the wide-eyed face of my adjutant Captain Simon. "Colonel, the British are here!" I followed him out and climbed the ramparts. Spread out in front of us were several large British man-of-wars. I looked around as my men raced to their stations. The day we dreaded was finally here.

"Captain, make sure that each battery has enough ammunition and the men are in place to meet the attack."

Just then, the unmistakable sound of cannons fire reverberated. I saw the puffs of smoke from the ships and followed the trace of the cannon balls as they descended on our position. There were loud crashes upon the impact of the shells. The shrieks of the wounded brought back a flood of terrible memories. My mind raced knowing that Fort Moultrie would play an important role protecting the harbor. I ran over to the gun crews and ordered them to return fire. I went from battery to battery to get a vantage point to detect if we were damaging the British fleet. There was so much smoke clouding my vision. It was difficult to gauge the accuracy of our guns. There was only the faint whisper of a breeze in my face.

The cannonade went on for hours. We sustained some damage but kept up a steady fire at the enemy. I could not detect the landing of British troops yet. The strategy was like that used against the French fort in Canada all those years ago. Soften up the defenses then send in the Army.

We were trapped in our little world. I had not heard from General Lincoln and had no idea if the British were attacking anywhere else along the coast. We would hold out as long as possible while trying to inflict as much damage as we could. I could never get used to sieges. It was harder being on the receiving end and the constant bombardment took its toll on all the defenders. This included me. There was a feeling of hopelessness enduring the constant explosions not knowing if you would take a direct hit. I had been through this more times than I would like to admit. Internally, I was rattled but I tried to maintain my calm and comfort the men, urging them on until the ordeal was over. One way or the other.

The shelling went on for weeks without a pause. We had done some damage to the British ships but hadn't sunk one yet. Unfortunately, some of those ships had slipped past our guns and went into Charleston harbor. This made our task of protecting the city more difficult. I was working in the blind and had no idea if the British had made a move inland to try and surround the beleaguered city. All we could do is hold out and continue to fight. I wondered how Anne and Beatrice were faring. It was comforting to know that they weren't in the city and should be safe from all of this.

Our supplies were holding up so far. How much longer would we have to fend off the British? I couldn't spare any of my men, but I decided to send a rider to Charleston to get an update from General Lincoln as to how the fight was going. We had to win this fight and keep the British out of South Carolina.

Chapter 48

Nigel Crittenden

Going Ashore

T he display of the heavy guns firing onto Charleston was awe-inspiring. It made me forget about my seasickness. I watched as the shells came down on the forts protecting the city. Would Smith be manning any of those defenses? That would make all that I had gone through worth my misery. While I stood there with my jaw agape, another officer came up beside me.

"What do you think, Crittenden?"

I took a sideways glance at the young man. He still looked pale from the journey. I think being on a boat at sea had taken more of a toll on him than me. "Lieutenant Anson, how are you today?"

He weakly grinned at me. "I shall be glad to set foot on land again."

I turned back to the spectacle. "It's a grand show of force. Hard to believe that the rebels think they can defeat the might of the Empire." We stood there in silence and continued to watch the destruction of the American defenses.

After days of witnessing the carnage, we were informed that the transport we were on would be sailing for the Edisto River where we would be disembarked. This would be part of the land portion of the invasion.

I couldn't wait to get on solid ground again. As we sailed up the river, it brought back memories of taking Savannah. The lush, swampy vegetation and the muggy air were reminders that this part of the colonies was unique. I had visions of the same victorious results. This could be a great leap toward ending this rebellion and going home. Of course, that could not be done until I took my revenge for my father's death.

We were sent ashore unmolested. There was chatter among the men at the lack of rebel fire. Still, there were a few potshots taken at us from covered positions. We marched inland and set up camp. I was told that we were on John's Island directly across from the city of Charleston. The city could be seen from our vantage point. The Navy continued its bombardment and the Americans weakly attempted to answer from guns placed on an island across from our position. The boom of the cannons reverberated throughout the harbor. I felt the percussion from where I stood as it rolled through my body. Smoke covered the water, but the explosions were brilliantly lit up against the backdrop of the city. It was exhilarating to witness. This was to be an even more glorious victory than that of capturing Savannah.

We settled in to await the inevitable orders to attach the American positions. I bit my lower lip with the thought that the barrage could also be taking a toll on the civilians in the area. It seemed improper to take the war to them. I suppose some had escaped once we set foot on land. A few Loyalists clung to our camp. They were a twitching, nervous group. I was uncomfortable around them as they would loudly proclaim their allegiance to the King. There was always a concern that these people could be spies for the rebels. I told the men to be tight-lipped at what they told those who inquired about our plans.

The men responded well to being given time to prepare for action while watching the daily bombardment. I received orders from Major Shenton to have my men assist in the building of earthworks on the west bank of the Ashley River that would accommodate cannons to add to the firepower. This was a difficult proposition due to the swampy land but it was a good distraction for the men.

The orders finally came at the end of March for us to man small boats that would ferry us across the Ashley River to the Charleston peninsula. By this time the Americans had pulled their defenses into the edge of the city. We were prepared for them to prevent us from crossing the wide river. Instead, they seemed to be more preoccupied with the British fleet that continued to rain down destruction on them. We reached the other side and started to entrench a series of fortifications north of the city. This effectively cut off Charleston from the rest of the colony. We continued to extend the trenches toward the outer defenses that the rebels had set up. Any fool could now see that it was only a matter of time. My men had not even fired a shot yet.

Chapter 49

Anne Smith

Back to Charleston

I hadn't wrapped my head around the death of the slave girl Bitsy when word reached Boone Hall that the British had begun their siege of Charleston. The news was especially hard for me. I was isolated here and Peter was in danger. Again. It was more than I could bear. I made twitchy movements as I paced around my bedroom. I knew I shouldn't make any rash decisions in this mood. I had to protect Beatrice and my unborn child. Going back to Charleston could be a disastrous choice, but I couldn't stay here while my husband could be harmed. Then there was the matter of Bitsy's death.

After some serious soul-searching, I decided that I would go to Peter. I spoke with Mary Toomer first. Even though we had our differences about the slavery issue, I owed her an explanation of why I was leaving. I found her in the parlor directing the staff for the day's chores. She was a handsome woman, raised in privilege. I came to admire her strength. Yet she was still beholden to her husband and the patriarchy of the South. I caught her attention, She smiled and then held up a finger. I waited patiently while she finished giving directions.

She had genuine concern on her drawn face. "Anne, you look ill. How can I help?"

I sucked in a deep breath. "Mary, you have been so kind to me and Beatrice. I feel safe here." I paused. "I need to go be with Peter now."

She raised a hand to her mouth and gasped. "Why would you put yourself in danger? The best thing you can do for Peter is to stay here with us."

I couldn't tell her about my feelings about what went on here at the plantation. "I appreciate your concern, but this is something that I need to do."

Mary's face remained contorted. "What about Beatrice?"

I stood firmly. "I will take her with me."

She mulled this over and nodded. "I will arrange transportation for you if this is something you must do."

An hour later, we were on our way. Beatrice and I rode in the back of a carriage driven by one of the slaves from the plantation. His name was Silas. He was an elderly man, run down by age and a hard life of labor. I was surprised that the Toomers trusted him to take me to Charleston and return. My attempts at small talk were rebuffed. Silas was polite but tight-lipped. I rode in silence for most of the twelve-mile journey.

The closer we got to the city, the more we encountered an exodus of the citizens fleeing the fighting. I gasped. *Am I too late?* When we reached the neck of the peninsula, we were stopped by armed Continental soldiers.

"Halt!"

Silas pulled the reins of the horse. The soldier came to the back of the carriage and looked intently at me. "What is your business here?"

I could hear the distant sound of explosions. I held Beatrice close to me. "Sir, I have come to be with my husband."

He cocked his head as if waiting for more. "Where is your husband?"

"He is an officer at Fort Moultrie. I am concerned about his safety."

"Ma'am, I don't believe that any of us are safe right now. You should not be here."

I tried to soften my facial features and smiled at the man turning on my charm. "I am here and don't intend on leaving. Can you direct me to General Lincoln's headquarters?"

He shrugged his shoulders and gave directions to Silas. The despair that I felt grew as we rode through the congested streets. There were signs of damage from the British shelling everywhere. There was a randomness to the damage. On one street, several structures were on fire. Then the next street was untouched. Smoke and ash flowed along like a fog carried on the wind. After some harrowing moments, we reached the Army's headquarters. Soldiers were hurrying off in different directions. I had trouble getting any of their attention. I climbed down from the carriage and stopped a man. His eyes were enlarged with fear. "Excuse me, sir, is General Lincoln available?"

He noticed me and squinted his eyes. He then threw this thumb over his shoulder and continued on his way. I walked up to the building that was the center of all the activity. When I tried to enter, I was stopped by a very serious-looking soldier. As I tried to plead my case, I heard my name being called. I looked up and saw a familiar-looking face. "Major Edwards, can you help me?"

He walked closer. "What are you doing here, Mrs. Smith?"

"I've come to check on my husband. Has there been any word?"

He gazed out in the direction of Fort Moultrie. "I'm afraid that we have not received any word from his command." He pointed toward the fort. "As you can see they are under attack as we speak."

I swiveled my body to look in that direction. "Is there any way for me to see him?"

"I can't afford to spare any men to escort you there right now. It's not safe for you here. You should go back to where you were."

I reached out and grabbed his arm. "That is not an option. Is there anywhere I can stay while I try to get word about Peter?"

He stopped and considered my question. "The British are about to surround us. There may not be any place safe to go. If you must stay, I would go north, away from the battery, to see if anyone will give you accommodations." With that, he was off.

I directed Silas to go in the direction that Major Edwards stated. We dodged both humans and shells maneuvering along the battery away from downtown. I watched in horror as the British ships in the harbor were throwing their deadly shells in our direction. It was utter chaos like the end of the world was coming upon us. Beatrice screamed with fear, reacting to the chaos and noise. I held her close while twisting my head seeking some place where we could stay. Silas stayed calm throughout the whole ordeal. I frantically called out to the people we passed looking for a boarding house. No one would stop to help. Then when things looked the bleakest, I spotted a sign hanging over one of the row houses on a side street, "Rooms to Let." I grabbed Silas and pointed in that direction.

I wasn't sure what I would find when I climbed the steps to the door. I knocked. After a few minutes, the front door cracked open. There stood a frazzled woman who was clearly in shock.

"Ma'am, I was hoping that you have lodging for my daughter and me." I pointed to Beatrice standing in the carriage.

She cocked her head and squinted her eyes. "Get your child and come in. Quickly!"

I ran back to the carriage and pulled Beatrice to me as Silas collected our bags. The woman ushered us inside. Silas placed the bags on the floor and headed back to the carriage.

"Silas, where are you going?"

He smirked. "Back home."

Chapter 50

Peter Smith

Hopeless

I began to despair as I frantically tried to rally my men. The shelling continued. There was little time to collect myself between volleys. I wasn't sure what was worse; the impact of the shell or the thunderous screaming sound they made. We did what we could to respond to the onslaught. Other than damaging a few of the British frigates, we were ineffective. The men were under constant stress. I could see the fear and despair in their faces. There was nowhere to hide. All they could do was to return fire and hope for the best. There was no help coming. My repeated attempts to get updates from General Lincoln went unanswered. We were on an island alone left to sink or swim it seemed. We had to hold out as long as possible. Hopefully, the soldiers in Charleston would be able to hold out and protect the city. As I stared out from my vantage point on the fort's wall, I had my doubts.

After a month of constant bombardment, I watched helplessly as the British fleet sailed past our position closer to Charleston. My head hung with the realization that the city was lost. We didn't dare fire on the enemy ships lest we hit the beleaguered city with our shells. My thoughts turned to how we could gather as many guns and ammunition as we could carry and make our escape before we were forced to surrender. It seemed like the prudent thing to do, but I had no orders authorizing such a movement. I agonized over having to await orders and our fate.

Five days later, we received word that General Lincoln had agreed to surrender the city of Charleston. This was one of the lowest points in my life. What would become of me and my men? Would I ever see Anne or Beatrice again? It was unbearable for me to consider that this was the end. All the sacrifices I had made would count for naught.

We waited dejectedly for the British to send troops to accept the surrender that was agreed to by Lt. Col. Scott. There were two hundred men and officers still manning the fort which had sustained serious damage in the fight. I stared blankly at the rubble thinking this is what our rebellion had come to, defeat after defeat. Some of the men had argued that we should continue to resist. However, it was bitterly clear that we were outnumbered and outgunned by the British. Nearly five hundred redcoats assembled outside the entrance of the garrison. The other officers and I led the men to surrender to the awaiting victors. It was humiliating to march past the smug faces of men who were my hated enemy. There was still a hint of rebellion on my face as I scowled at the victors. We were ordered to stack our arms and line up to be escorted back to Charleston as prisoners of war.

As we shuffled our feet in a long line, meandering along the dirt path that led from the fort off the island, our arrogant foes taunted us. One of the catcalls was directed at me.

"Look, Albert, they have jolly well scrapped the barrel using a one-armed man to fight the King's grand army." There was a smattering of laughter at my expense.

We were herded over to the neck of the Charleston isthmus where the enlisted men were separated and taken off from my view. Those men, who I had spent so much time with, had fear etched on their faces. I was concerned for their safety. When the men were out of earshot, a large, beefy sergeant told the remaining group of officers, "We have a special place for your kind."

I furrowed my brow thinking, *What did he mean?*

There were British soldiers everywhere as we walked the narrow cobbled streets of Charleston. It never occurred to me that I would be recognized for the role I played in the American naval victory over my old ship HMS Progress. That didn't seem to be important at this very moment. Our captors led us down House Street. The street was lined with elegant row houses and shocked citizens watching the debacle. I was too embarrassed to look up at the people who witnessed us in our time of bondage. I felt shame for letting them down.

From House Street, we made a left turn onto Broad Street. At the end of Broad, there stood the Exchange building. The closer we got to the building, the more I was resigned to the fact that it would be my new home. The structure was a two-story brick building with Greek columns framing windows on the top floor. I looked up to see that it was topped by a cupola. We were halted in the front, near a stairway. The same obnoxious sergeant announced, "Gentlemen, welcome to your new home."

That was only the beginning of our horror. We were unceremoniously herded down to the bowels of the building to a red brick-lined basement. I squinted to try and see the layout of the cramped room. The brick columns hid what appeared to be catacombs. I wondered how many poor souls were already here. It was stuffy and already in the process of being overcrowded with prisoners. The stench of human waste was overpowering. Worse than anything I experienced while serving on naval ships. The limited lighting came from barred slits of windows around the perimeter of the basement. I was shoved into the space and when the door was slammed shut, it was nearly pitch dark. That's when I heard the screams from the other prisoners. I added my voice to those screams as I tried to endure the darkened, claustrophobic prison.

Chapter 51

Nigel Crittenden

Victory

We completely cut off Charleston from the mainland. Strategically placed trenches were dug to get closer to the outer defenses of the rebels. There was sporadic fire of cannons and muskets from the Americans. It was more a hindrance than anything. The men were hard at work building trenches that were perpendicular to the enemy works. Little by little, we edged closer. The sound of the bombardment could still be heard echoing from the ships in the harbor. It was only a matter of time now.

There were rampant rumors that passed through the ranks that the rebels were trying to surrender. It only made the men work harder at extending the trenches. I had not received any word of a possible surrender. I couldn't believe the ease at which we closed on the enemy. We had not taken any serious casualties. It was like the battle for Savannah all over again.

The next morning, the sound of shrieking shells could be heard. I jumped up and watched them arching toward the center of town. I followed the trajectory of the missiles as they landed and did their ghastly work. This must be a new strategy. Up until now, the assault had been directed at the city's defenses. I wondered what caused the decision to destroy the city. This went on throughout the morning until white flags could be seen waving from the American lines. A chorus of cheers rang out from the men in the trenches. It was over. We had captured the prize of the Southern colonies. Surely this was the beginning of the end of the rebellion. I was overjoyed and wiped my brow with the back of my hand. The reality of the situation sunk in and I collapsed to my knees while the men around me celebrated. I had little sleep over the past week and it had taken its toll on me.

We were ordered to move into the city and gather up American prisoners. I was shocked at the sight of our so-called "enemy." They were a ragtag group of men who looked as exhausted as I was. I stood back and crossed my arms over my chest as my men roughly manhandled the prisoners into a line. The victors hurled insults at the defeated soldiers. I did nothing to stop my men from venting their frustrations at the helpless souls. I reasoned that they brought this on themselves by standing up to the King.

We received orders to disarm the prisoners and march them down to the waterfront. The decision had been made to take the enlisted men out to barges that were anchored in the harbor. The officers were to be taken to the Exchange building where a makeshift prison had been set up in the basement. It didn't concern me where these men were to be imprisoned.

There was a fog covering my brain from lack of sleep and I shuffled my feet in step with the men around me. I tried to shake the cobwebs when we entered the city. I was impressed by the layout of Charleston. Tidy little squares with lines of homes surrounding manicured parks. There were signs of damage from the shelling, but this was a lovely city. I was surprised by the number of citizens who turned out to watch us parade past them. The people were made up of women, children, the elderly and slaves who had the looks of shock on their faces from the continued shelling. They remained silent as we passed. I fought the urge to yell at them for what they started. I collected my composure and thought better of it.

It suddenly came to me...Smith. Could he possibly be here? The odds seemed insurmountable. A feeling came over me that he was. I perked up. Looking around carefully at the gathered crowd, where do I start? I left the column and walked toward a group of women. "Do any of you know an American officer named Peter Smith?"

The women stood there with open mouths, but there was a look of pure hatred emanating from them. Not one of them responded. I continued. "He is missing his left arm." Still no response. I clenched my fists and yelled at them. "Someone must know this man!"

The women cowered at the sound of my shouting. I was undeterred. I continued to confront the people lined up on the streets. Still nothing. Then it hit me. I went back to the line of prisoners and looked for signs of rank among the mass of rebels. I noticed a man who wore epaulets with the rank of major. He took in my stare and then averted his eyes. I pushed my way to the man. "Major, do you know Peter Smith?"

At first, he did not respond. I continued to grill him. He slowly looked up at me. "I heard tell of a hero who was missing his left arm."

Adrenaline pulsed through my veins. "Where is he?"

The major stepped back from the force of my voice. He had the unmistakable look of defeat on his face. In a weak, muted voice he replied. "I have not seen the man. I just heard that he was here in Charleston."

I pushed away from the mass of men and continued to question everyone I saw. No one else knew of Smith.

We reached the piers at the southern end of the city. There was a mass of prisoners who were being herded onto small boats to be taken out to the barges. We turned over our enlisted rebels and gathered a dozen officers in our charge. I ordered most of my men to stay and help with the enlisted prisoners while I picked three men to go with me to escort the officers to the Exchange building. If Smith was in Charleston, that's where he would be.

I led the small procession down Broad Street. My pace quickened the closer we got. I had tunnel vision. This could be the moment that I was waiting for. I got to the makeshift prison well ahead of our prisoners. There was a table set up at the front of the building. A rotund captain was checking in the prisoners and looked to be scribing their information on a ledger. I shifted my weight from foot to foot while waiting for my turn. When I got to the table, the captain looked up at me. "What is it, Lieutenant?"

I straightened my uniform and pointed over my shoulder. "I have some prisoners for you."

He looked around me. "Very well. Have your men line them up."

I cleared my throat. He looked back at me with disgust. "What is it?"

I was wondering if you have a Peter Smith imprisoned here?"

He tilted his head. "What is this man to you, Lieutenant?"

I debated telling him the truth. I paused, then said, "He is responsible for my father's death."

The captain sat back in his chair. He raised his eyebrows but did not ask any questions. I watched as he leaned forward and read through the ledger. My anticipation grew as he turned each page. When he got to the end, he shook his head. "No one by that name has been logged in the ledger."

I deflated and started to turn. "We only started checking in prisoners yesterday. There were already a number of the enemy down in the hold before then."

I nearly fell over, turned back and faced him, "Is there any way that I would be allowed to go down there and see for myself?"

"I don't see why not." He turned to one of the armed guards standing behind him. "Jeffers, escort the Lieutenant down to the hold to look for his prisoner."

My stomach was turning over as I followed Jeffers. We got to the entrance and he led me down into the poorly lit space. I gasped and put my hand over my mouth. The scene below me was horrific. There were prisoners stuffed into every corner of the compact room. The smell of death and human waste was overpowering. How would I find him? Jeffers turned to look at me for direction. I grabbed a handkerchief and placed it over my mouth and nose and shooed him forward.

It was dark and hard to make out features of the poor souls entombed here. I called out "Peter Smith, are you here?" I stepped over the mass of people lying on the cold, bricked floor. "Have any of you seen a one-armed man?" No response.

The deeper we got into the prison, the darker it was. I continued to call out. I grew frustrated and lashed out, even kicking those in my way. Jeffers kept quiet, but I could make out a glare on his darkened face. I continued on until we reached the other end of the room. No sign of my nemesis. I hung my head and grabbed Jeffers' sleeve. "Let's get out of this unholy place."

He led me back to the light of the open door. When we stepped back into daylight, I removed the handkerchief and took in deep breaths of fresh air.

This would not be the end of my search.

Chapter 52

Peter Smith

Hell on Earth

My despair had reached alarming depths. I reminded myself that I had so much to live for, but how could I possibly last for an indeterminate amount of time in this hell on earth? Each day brought more prisoners. There wasn't enough room for the ones that were already here. We were not provided with enough food or fresh water. The cries and pleas from my fellow inmates made sleep hard to come by. This place reminded me of the prison I was in back in England as a young boy. At least there we had sunlight and meals.

There was no rhyme or reason to when the guards would bring down food, or carry out dead prisoners. As far as I could tell, there was only one entrance in and out. There were tiny slits in the brick wall near the ceiling that allowed some light and air to get in, but they were not big enough for a man to squeeze through. There wasn't enough fresh air flowing through those windows to replace the foul stagnant air we were forced to breathe. Somehow, I had to keep my mind sharp and figure out a way out of this predicament. Sitting in a corner of the deathtrap, I tried hard to picture Anne's and Beatrice's faces. It would be the memory of them that would keep the fire burning for me to survive this latest setback.

I tried to talk to the other inmates locked away in this dungeon. Most had already given up and were resigned to their fate. What makes men behave like animals and treat their fellow humans in this manner? I had to find more like-minded men to help me with my escape. There just had to be a way out.

On the third day of my captivity, it was hard to keep track of the days, another batch of prisoners were brought in. I just happened to be at the very back of the room going hand over hand trying to find a weakness to exploit. There was a commotion going on and I could hear yelling. I was curious about all the fuss and I carefully tried to make my way back toward the sound. It was difficult to avoid the bodies of the other inmates, so I went slowly. Then the blood drained from my face when I heard, "Are you here, Peter Smith?"

Who could be looking for me? By the tone of the voice, it probably wasn't someone trying to rescue me. Panic overcame me. I turned and scrambled back to where I was. There were cries of pain from someone I accidentally stepped on. I froze waiting to see if that voice would get closer. There was a moment of silence. I continued. When I got to the back corner, I snatched a tattered blanket and got into a tight ball and covered myself. This instantly made me flashback to that same prison in Portsmouth and the day that the sailors carried me off to serve on the HMS Progress.

It was a harrowing few minutes cowering under that blanket waiting to see if I would be caught. I gulped in a stale lungful of air and held my breath when I heard that voice close to me. Just as I couldn't hold my breath anymore, I heard, "Let's get out of this unholy place."

I took another deep breath and almost went into a coughing spasm as the man walked away. Who was that and why were they looking for me? One of my fellow officers, Franklin McCall, who I served with at the fort, crawled over to me. "Peter, what was that all about?"

"I have no earthly idea."

He grunted. "He sounded angry."

I racked my brain. Maybe it was a survivor from the Progress. How could they possibly know that I was here? I would have to be more cautious. I turned toward Franklin. "We need to get away from this place. I don't want to die here."

I couldn't see his face, but he grunted again.

Chapter 53

Anne Smith

Finding Husbands

The disheveled woman grabbed my bag and led me upstairs without a word. I scanned the narrow house as I climbed the stairs. When I got to the top, the woman stood by an open door. I peeked around her to see a modest room with a single bed, bureau and desk. I smiled at her. "Thank you for taking us in on such short notice."

She stared at me with dull brown eyes. An explosion outside made both of us jump.

"Why are you here? You should have taken your child and gone far from this place."

I gently put Beatrice down and walked to the woman. I could see that she was scared and I placed my hands on her arms. "My name is Anne Smith. My husband is among the defenders of Charleston and I had to see if he is still alive."

She crumpled into my arms and began to sob. "My husband is also out there somewhere and I have not heard any news."

I held her tightly and stroked her hair. "We shall need to be strong for each other and find out where our husbands are."

As we got settled into our new residence, I learned that our host's name was Martha Holmes. Her husband, Jonathan, was recruited by the local militia to man the defenses north of town. She hung the sign for renters to bring in extra income while he was away. She had the foresight to stock up on supplies before the British took over, but they wouldn't last forever.

We spent each day locked away in the cramped house while we watched events that transpired outside. There was a lot of activity. British soldiers walked through the streets maintaining order. I stared out the front window to look for any indication of prisoners being taken away. My nerves were frazzled, needing to know anything about the fate of Peter. Beatrice remained oblivious to the events taking place. This was comforting to me until she waddled over to me and said, "Want Dada."

On the morning of the third day, we agreed to go outside and get some news. We would stay together for protection. As we stepped out onto the street, we peered around carefully. It was a typically hot, muggy spring day. There was little activity on the street. We decided to go south toward the Battery. I carried Beatrice and followed Martha as she hugged the buildings along the way. We went around a corner at House Street and Union Street. Martha let out an audible gasp and stood frozen in place. I peeked around her and saw the results of the indiscriminate shelling. A row of homes were destroyed and the embers from the resulting fire still sparked and flashed. No one tried to put out the fire and black smoke gently rose from the damage and floated off with the wind.

The closer we got to the pier, the more activity we saw. There were British soldiers everywhere. They kept an eye on us but must have determined that we weren't a threat. Something didn't seem right to me. Then it hit me. Where are all the townspeople? I spotted an elderly gentleman walking alone in the opposite direction. I headed toward him. "Sir, can I ask you a question?"

He was startled by my request and turned his head to see if anyone was watching. He raised an eyebrow and closed the gap between us. "How may I assist you, madam?"

I pointed to Martha. Both of us are trying to find out what happened to our husbands."

He stood back a step. "Would they be Rebels or British?"

I suddenly felt very vulnerable. He must be a Tory. "They would be American soldiers."

The men let out a snort. "They should have made better choices. I heard that most of the prisoners are out of those ships in the bay." He pointed out past the seawall to the harbor. "The others are in the basement of the Exchange building on Bay Street." He turned around and walked off.

I looked at Martha. "There isn't much we can do if they are on those ships. I say we try our luck at the Exchange building." She nodded her head and we set off. When we got to Bay Street, we got a better view of all the British ships in the harbor. The show of strength made me depressed. I forced my legs to carry me to the large building that was our destination. When we reached the building, we saw a myriad of activities. Beatrice was getting fidgety and hard to hold. I was drenched in sweat and must have smelled horrible. Martha was overwhelmed and stood behind me.

I boldly walked up to a British soldier guarding the entrance. He stood at attention and only glared at me. "I would like to see if my husband is here." He blew a breath out and with his eyes directed me to the side of the building. I gave Beatrice to Martha and strode in that direction. When I turned the corner, I saw more soldiers. I walked up to the man that looked to be in charge. He cocked his head. "Madam, you should not be here."

I tried to soften my features and turned on my charm. Batting my eyes, I said, "Sir, I was advised that my husband is possibly locked in your prison. My daughter and I are desperate for any information you can provide."

The man moved sideways to look behind me at Martha and Beatrice, then back to me. He scanned up and down taking in my body. There was a danger in the way he looked at me. "Why should I be inclined to help a traitor or his wife?"

"I beg you sir for any information."

He considered my request. "What is his name?"

I was hopeful. "Peter Smith. He is missing his left arm."

The man turned toward the other soldiers who all shrugged their shoulders. It doesn't appear that he is here.

My shoulders dropped. "Is there any way I can look to see if he is here?"

He became short with me and with a gruff voice stated, "Today is not a good day. Come back at another time. Maybe we can accommodate your request for a favor."

I knew exactly what he meant by that. We walked away dejected. Martha handed Beatrice back and whispered, "I didn't get to ask about Jonathan."

We walked back to Martha's home in silence.

Chapter 54

Nigel Crittenden
Tedious Duty

After going through the emotions of capturing Charleston, it was back to the same old tedious occupation duty. I had too much free time and wandered through the streets of Charleston. Other than the damage inflicted by the siege, it was a beautiful city. I came to understand that it is one of the oldest cities in the colonies. I was amazed at the wealth that was displayed. I supposed that we were the biggest steward of that wealth by purchasing goods from these people. There were several slaves who were already put to work repairing the battle damage. I bit my lower lip while I watched these poor souls toil under a steamy sun. There wasn't a hint of joy on their faces as they went about their business. How can a benevolent God allow this to happen? Maybe the best thing that could come out of putting down the rebellion would be to end the practice. I suppose that was an unrealistic wish as too many people prospered from their labor. On both sides of the Atlantic.

There was an edginess from the local citizens that I didn't encounter in New York or even Savannah. It almost bordered on outright hostility. It must be from the years that they were allowed to live without a strong controlling hand from the King. Of course, there were a few Loyalists who came out of hiding once we captured the city. I still looked upon them as a needy group with intentions that didn't appear to be in the best interests of the King and Empire. They were only motivated by what was best for them. I could see them trading their loyalty back to the Rebels if it suited them.

I couldn't shake the feeling that I missed something when I inspected the dungeon at the Exchange building. I shuddered at the memory of that place. It was ghastly. I reminded myself that the inhabitants were traitors and deserved a traitor's death. Still, it bothered me the conditions they endured. I guess it was no worse than the men who were locked below in the transport ships in the harbor. War is a nasty business. I see little glory in the killing of fellow Christians. I stopped my train of thought, that is except for killing Peter Smith.

There was a strong pull for me to go back to the Exchange and search that dungeon again. I was told that the Rebel officers were assigned there and the enlisted men to the ships in the harbor. It would have to wait as I was assigned to command men in the northern part of the city who were stationed to protect against any Rebel raids. Apparently, several Americans had made it out of our trap and were raiding British forts throughout South Carolina. I was informed that a series of installations were strategically set up to move supplies and men to capture the entire colony. I heard that men had been sent out to Camden, Ninety-Six, and Augusta, Georgia. I knew that it was a matter of time until I would be sent to one of those or other posts. I couldn't wait too long to go back one more time and see if Smith was locked up in Charleston. I needed some good luck, especially after all I had done to get to this point. Then I could go back to England and tell my mother that I had dispatched the man responsible for my father's death.

Chapter 55

Peter Smith

Death of a Friend

My concept of time came to a halt as each day melted into another. The only way to tell if it was night or day was to look out the tiny, barred windows for sunlight. There was so much death and disease in this place. Many of the inhabitants had given up and waited to die and their wasted bodies carted out. I refused to give up. Each day I made a plan to get through the day. This included making sure that I ate and got some water. At times I had to fight with the other prisoners just to fulfill the most basic needs. I would muscle my way toward the entrance each morning to make sure I got some moldy bread. There were times that I would steal my rations from another prisoner who was as wretched as me. Desperation can make a person deteriorate to their primal self. I wasn't proud of what I had to do to survive.

Another part of my plan each day was trying to figure out a way to escape this dungeon alive. I sought out and befriended other prisoners who were as mentally strong as I was. We would spend hours discussing and plotting a way to break out from our hell. In the back corner of the prison, the bricks were loose and we would spend hours trying to work them free with whatever tool we could find. It was slow, methodical work and I feared that we could weaken the wall enough for it to collapse on us. Maybe that wouldn't be a bad thing.

For the most part, the British guards left us alone. I think they were afraid to come down among us. Each time they made cursory inspections, the mass of dead and dying would plead to let them go. It was a harrowing experience to be among such suffering all in the name of punishing us for being rebellious. I believed that the guards were sadistic and I would have loved to strangle the life out of them. I'm sure my fellow inmates shared the same feeling. In our weakened states, it was doubtful we could have put up much of a fight. They even made the prisoners carry out the dead.

Franklin McCall had been with me from the beginning. He was a strong man with as much of a will to live as I had. During the second or third week of our captivity, we were working at removing bricks when he suddenly doubled over in pain. The sun's last rays were shining down on us from above casting a surreal orange glow, but it was hard to see his face. I reached over and touched his back. "Franklin, what is happening?" Then the unmistakable smell of human waste overpowered me. I pulled away from him. The bloody flux. He was as good as dead.

He lay there in his waste groaning. My mind raced as to what I should do. There had been many deaths due to this cruel malady. I reasoned that it was caused by the putrid food and water we were given. I couldn't allow myself to catch it from him. I must survive for Anne and Beatrice. Still, I had to do what I could to make my comrade as comfortable as possible. I called out to anyone who might help me. I only heard the sound of scurrying as they tried to distance themselves from Franklin.

I moved back toward him and could feel heat resonating off his body and the involuntary shaking that went along with the progression of the disease. I felt around for something to cover him up with. My right hand grasped a piece of canvas. When I started to pull it, the unmistakable sound of squealing and scurrying feet could be heard. Rats. I shuddered and continued to drag the tarp over to the prone body of my friend. I wrapped him up in the canvas and tried to say soothing words to him. Franklin continued to moan throughout the night. I stayed there with him until dawn, when he took his last gasp of air. I was angry and started to drag him toward the entrance into this hell hole. I struggled with only my right arm and didn't care who I bumped into. I stopped when I reached the stairs. I stood there for a couple of minutes and mumbled, "May God have mercy on your soul." Then I turned and slunk back into the darkness.

Each day, I become more desperate. The work to remove the loose bricks wasn't getting me any closer to escaping. There had to be a better way. There began to be more of a cadence to when the guards would open the door, have the dead bodies removed and then food and water were sent down. If I was going to do something bold, it would need to be during this time when the guards were distracted. My body ached and my mind started to wander from lack of fresh water and food. I had trouble concentrating. I forced myself to picture Anne in my mind to make me stronger. I refused to die in this dungeon.

There hadn't been any new prisoners brought down in some time, but there were a few prisoners that had been removed. I heard talk from the other inmates that some important men had been discovered rotting down here. They were rumored to be signers of the Declaration of Independence. I never heard their names or where they were being sent. There were also women and children imprisoned. I had yet to see any for myself. Had the war come to this where even the weak among us were to be treated like criminals?

I realized that there was little chance that I would be recognized as someone important by the British, so the only other way to leave was by dying. That wasn't an option. I had to find a way to escape. My hatred for the British grew each day. This hate and my desire to see Anne fueled me and probably kept me alive. Giving up any chance of tunneling to my freedom, I reasoned that I would need to fake my death to escape this place. How would I be able to pull that off?

Chapter 56

Anne Smith

A Miracle

We were dejected as we retraced our path back to the boarding house. I mourned for both of us. Martha didn't even get the chance to check the status of her husband. We collapsed on the couch in the sitting room and Martha sobbed uncontrollably. Beatrice looked at me for an answer. It broke my heart to see the look on my daughter's face. I had to stay strong for all of us. I picked her up and rocked her in my lap as Matha continued to wail.

When Martha had gotten control of herself, I turned to her and in the strongest voice I could muster, said, "We must not give up. We will continue to search until we find our husbands."

She wiped her eyes and I had to turn away from the helpless look on her face. "It will take a miracle for that to happen. You heard those soldiers, they couldn't care less about us or our husbands." She put her face into her hands and began to sob again.

"We will have to make our own miracle and give those soldiers a reason to want to help us."

Her mouth dropped open and her red-rimmed eyes widened. "How can we do that?"

I pursed my lips together as my mind churned. "We are two resourceful women. We will find a way."

The next morning, we strode with determination back to the Exchange building. I was raised in a very conservative religious home, raised by a pastor, but I would use my femininity to my advantage. I would do what was necessary to find my husband. I prepared for this possibility by accentuating my bosom and shortening my dress above my ankles. I laughed when I saw the shocked face of Martha at my appearance. She even looked down at her dress and then shrugged her shoulders. Well, at least I could count on her to watch Beatrice while I tried to charm my way into that prison.

While we strode toward the prison, I noticed that the city seemed to be calmer by the expression on the people's faces. They had resigned themselves to the new reality. I took this as a bad sign. Didn't they understand what was at stake? I thought to myself that I would never go back to being ruled by a king that didn't care about me or my family. Surely, I couldn't be the only one in Charleston to see this. I was shaken in my core, but as we rounded the corner and could see our destination, I composed myself for the task at hand. It was midmorning, already the heat was building and storm clouds in the distance promised rain. There was little activity going on around the building. I couldn't decide if this was a good or bad thing. I had Martha stay back with Beatrice and as I pulled down the bodice and pushed up my bosom, I sauntered over to the two guards with a seductive smile on my lips.

One of the guards noticed me and poked an elbow into the other's side to get his attention. Fortunately, they weren't the same guards who were on duty yesterday. The closer I got, they just stood there gawking.

"Gentlemen, I was wondering if you could do me a small favor?" I paused while they stumbled over each other trying to impress me.

One of the men tipped his hat. "What could we possibly do for you, Mum?"

I batted my eyes. "There is a man down in your prison who is not supporting his daughter." I pointed over to Beatrice. "I wanted to talk to him about where he is keeping the money we need to survive."

Instantly, both of their faces turned serious. I may have overplayed my hand. "We are not allowed to let anyone down there." The guard held out his rifle in my direction. I saw the other guard stare at Beatrice and then back to me. He reached out and pushed the rifle barrel to the ground. "Mum, you don't want to go down there. There is only death and disease in that place." I started to say something, but he just gently shook his head.

My eyes welled up with tears as I turned and started to walk away. That was my best and only option to see if Peter is here. Martha saw everything. "What do we do now?"

I took Beatrice from her. "There has to be someone we can talk to. I refuse to give up." Something caught my attention and I looked down and noticed that there were barred windows at ground level. I was intrigued. I looked back to make sure the guards weren't watching and walked around to the side of the building. More windows. There was a tree that blocked the view from the street. My heart started to thump in my chest as I edged over to one of the windows. Martha had a confused look on her face but followed me. I put Beatrice down and got on my hands and knees. I tried to look into the darkness of the room to see if I could make out any faces.

The smell was atrocious and I had to cover my nose. As my eyes adjusted, I noticed there was some movement.

"Peter Smith, are you down there?" I heard some groans but no one responded. I cleared my throat and in a louder voice I pleaded, "Peter Smith, please answer me!" When it seemed hopeless, a face appeared. I pulled back from the sudden sight. I saw a filthy face of a man covered by an unkempt beard and open sores across his face.

"Who are you looking for?" His eyes darted and he tried to cover them from the sunlight.

"Peter Smith. He was an officer at Fort Moultrie."

The man thought about it and his face was blank.

I suddenly had a revelation. "He's missing his left arm."

The man put a finger in the air. "Wait right there." Then he was gone.

Martha bent down. "Did you ask him about Jonathan?"

I turned toward her and shook my head. "I will when he comes back."

We sat there for a few minutes. I could hear voices and shouts below. Just then, the sky became dark and there was the crack of a lightning strike which made us jump. Please hurry before it rains.

I noticed that someone was coming over to the window. I took a glance at the street. No one was watching. The dark figure came closer and he grabbed the bar on the window to pull himself up. The anticipation was killing me. I saw the top of the mystery man's head start to appear when another crash of thunder shook the building. I fell back as did the man in the dungeon. Beatrice cried and Martha tried to console her. I had to know who this man was.

He attempted to pull himself up again. This time I began to get a look at his face. "My God, Peter it is you!"

The man rapidly blinked his eyes as if trying to focus. He locked onto my face. "Anne, how is it that you are here?"

I cried out in joy. "I feared that I would never find you. How can I get you out of there?" He twisted his neck, still not sure this was happening. Another flash of lightning. Close. "Peter, Beatrice is here with me." I reached back and grabbed my daughter. "Look, it's Daddy." Peter was holding tight to the bar and couldn't reach out and touch either of us. I put my hand on his and gently stroked his fingers.

"The only way for me to leave is to pretend that I'm dead. The British have the dead taken out every morning right after dawn. Come back then and bring me some fresh clothes. Try to cause a distraction so that they don't check to see that I am truly dead. I will make my way back behind the building and go to the pier to hide. Then meet up with me and we will make our escape."

"Do you think that will work?"

"It's the only chance I have. I am dying down here."

Just as I started to get up, the rain came crashing down in sheets. Martha grabbed my shoulder. "Jonathan." I turned back to the window and shouted above the roar of the storm. "Peter, do you know if Jonathan Holmes is down there with you?"

He shrugged and mouthed, "I will try to find him."

We huddled together and ran to find cover from the rain. A miracle indeed.

Chapter 57

Peter Smith

Escape

When I heard my name being called, it was like something out of a dream. I'm not a religious man, but thoughts of an angel coming to carry my soul away came to mind. There couldn't possibly be anyone who knew I was down here. I put off the first mention of my name as a hallucination. The second time got my attention and I perked up. It sounded like it came from one of the windows on the far side of the room. I started to crawl in that direction like a moth attracted to a flame. I tried not to climb over the others that lay in my path, but it was nearly impossible. About the time I got to the wall, another prisoner stood above me. "Are you Smith?"

I strained to look up at him. "Peter Smith."

The dark figure threw his thumb over his shoulder. "Someone is looking for you."

I felt anticipation mixed with fear. When I reached the wall, I pulled myself up into a sitting position. I felt very weak and looked up at the window. It might have well been a mile away. I caught my breath and looked around for something to climb on. There was a wooden barrel standing next to me. With every ounce of strength I had left, I pulled myself up and slowly climbed onto the barrel. There was a sense of urgency as I reached up with my right hand to grasp the bar on the window. Ever so slowly, I pulled myself up to take a look. A sudden flash of lightning followed by a crack of thunder nearly made me fall off my perch.

I regained my composure and stood up straight to peer over the edge of the window. At first, I wasn't sure what I saw. It looked like the angel that came for me. I must be dead. I tried to clear my vision when I heard the angel shout, "My God, Peter it is you." In my wildest dreams, I never expected her to find me. Then she placed Beatrice by the window and I cried dry tears. I couldn't reach out and touch them. Seeing my family gave me the strength to keep going. I quickly decided that faking my death was the only option and I shared the plan with Anne. She voiced her concerns, but it was the only way. The rain started coming down and I sent her off. Before she got up to leave, she cried out about finding Jonathan Holmes. I continued to watch until they were out of sight. Who was Jonathan Holmes?

The rest of the plan came to me as I carefully made my way across the darkened dungeon floor. I would take the clothes from someone who already died. The smell alone should prevent the guards from checking too closely. I would try to get as close as I could to the door and wait for the morning to come. As a second thought, I called out for any information on Jonathan Holmes. No one admitted to knowing him. I didn't have a description of the man or where he fought. This made it nearly impossible to find him in this dank death trap.

I was exhausted beyond belief when I pulled myself up to the bottom of the brick stairs at the base of the door. The storm outside was making itself known and water came rushing down into the dungeon that was below sea level. The water felt magnificent but I was concerned that it would wash away the smell of death I was counting on. I held the scraps of clothes I collected over my head to keep them dry. Then I settled in, waiting for dawn.

I must have dozed off. I was awoken by the sound of rustling keys in the door. I spun my head back and forth panicking. There were still puddles of water on the grimy floor, but I somehow managed to keep the clothes dry. I quickly stripped off my clothes and slipped the blood and shit-stained shirt over my head. There was no movement around me and I laid back on the floor just as the door swung open. I prayed that I looked as bad as I felt. I slightly opened my eyes and my mouth hung open. Once I heard footsteps coming near, I held my breath.

"Check that one. He looks dead."

I felt rough hands grabbing my head. I desperately needed to take a breath.

"He's dead alright. I shall never get used to the smell. You two, come here and carry this man out."

I felt myself being lifted and took the chance at being caught by slowly taking in a deep breath of air.

"Take him and put him in that wagon."

The next sensation was floating on air and then landing roughly on a flat surface. I couldn't risk looking around to see if Anne was there. I lay still waiting for something to happen when another body was tossed on top of me. I wasn't expecting it and nearly screamed out. Unable to move, I felt claustrophobic, nearly losing control of my faculties. Still no signs of a diversion. What would happen when they took me to be buried? There was some shouting, then another body was thrown on me.

"That's all for today."

The wagon started to move. My eyes flew open. Did I miss my chance?

Chapter 58

Anne Smith

Diversion

We huddled under the awning of a dry goods shop trying to keep out of the elements. There was a river of water running down the street carrying away debris. I was soaked to the bone and felt the trembling body of Beatrice clinging to me. I couldn't believe that I found Peter still alive. I hated to leave him in that place. I tried to recall all the words that he said, but I couldn't get past his admission that he was dying. I feared for him and was concerned about his plan to escape. How would I be able to aid in getting him out of that horrible place? He wasn't clear about that part of the plan.

We stayed under that awning for an hour until the storm passed and the sun's rays fought to break through the thick bands of clouds. I looked out at the street and noticed that the floodwaters had receded. Steam eerily rose from the wet street. Beatrice had fallen asleep in my arms. I turned my attention to Martha. She was rubbing her sides with her arms and was staring off into the distance. "Martha, we should go back to your home."

That seemed to snap her out of her trance. "Do you think your husband will find out where Jonathan is?"

"He will do everything he can." I turned to walk up the street and she followed me.

We changed into dry clothes and sat in front of a fire that I started in the fireplace. I was mesmerized by the flames and looked deeply at the bright colors. My mind churned with what I would do to help Peter. I would never forgive myself if I couldn't help him gain his freedom. I titled my head down to watch Beatrice chew on a piece of dried bread. Then there was an unexpected flutter in my stomach. The baby kicked. With all that was going on, I forgot I was pregnant. I was glad that I didn't tell Peter. He already has enough to be concerned with.

I'm not sure what woke me. I was lying on the floor next to the fireplace. The fire was out. There were only a few smoking embers left. I stretched my arms and tried to work a kink out of my back. Beatrice was curled up in a ball next to me. I looked over my shoulder to see Martha on the couch. I saw a flicker of light come through the front window. I bolted upright and searched for the clock. It was 5:30. I blew out a lung full of air. There was still time.

As quiet as a mouse, I got up and went into the kitchen to get something to eat. My dreams were filled with all that could go wrong today. The one thing I knew was that I would leave Beatrice with Martha and go by myself. At 6:00 I woke up Martha.

"I'm going to go help Peter. Would you look after Beatrice until we get back?"

She was groggy as she listened to me. "Yes, dear. Be safe and see if you can find anything about Jonathan."

I squeezed her shoulder, took a last look at Beatrice and scurried through the front door. There were still dark shadows on the streets as I increased my pace. There was some tree debris in the roadway from the storm. There were also puddles of water that had spooled. I still tried to work out what

I would do to cause a diversion. What if the same guards were on duty? I would have to improvise. When I turned the corner onto Broad Street, I could see the sun had broken over the horizon. It painted the sky a deep red. Peter said to be there at sunrise. Was I too late?

I started to run. There was activity in the front of the building. A wagon was being loaded by two men who were barely clothed. I couldn't make out what they were putting in the back of the wagon. I started to slow down as I was out of breath. As I got closer, my mouth dropped open and I stopped in my tracks. They were loading bodies. I was too late.

The wagon started to move up Bay Street. I quickly scanned around and noticed there were few people on the streets. I wasn't sure where they were taking the bodies, but I would have to cut them off. The old man driving the wagon didn't appear to be in a hurry, so I had some time. I turned around and took a left turn at State Street. My lungs ached as I tried to keep up a steady pace. When I reached a narrow alleyway, I took a glance to my right to see if the wagon had passed. No sign. Could they have turned toward the piers? I ran down the alley toward Cordes Street and when I got to the intersection with Bay, I saw the wagon make a right onto Cordes. I crossed Bay following it.

Out of desperation, I called out, "Sir, can you stop." The man pulled back on the reins of the horse and swiveled his head in my direction. I slowed and looked for anyone who could be following me. The driver stared at me as I closed the distance. When I got to the back of the wagon, I glanced sideways to see if Peter was in the back. I nearly jumped when he winked at me.

I walked up to the man and leaned over to catch my breath. "Sir, thank you for stopping. I am desperately trying to find my daughter. She ran away this morning and I was hoping that you had seen her."

He scratched his head and shrugged his shoulders. "No, Mum."

There was a rattling from the back of the wagon. As the driver tried to turn back to look what the cause was, I grabbed his arm. "Are you sure that you did not see her? She must have come this way." That did the trick. His attention returned to me. Out of the corner of my eye, I saw Peter lower himself from the back of the wagon. He then disappeared behind a deserted shack.

"I'm sorry for troubling you, kind sir. I won't bother you anymore."

The man tipped his hat and snapped the reins to continue his journey. I stood there watching him disappear around the corner and went looking for Peter. I found him cowering behind some bushes. He saw me and jumped up to hug me. It felt so good to feel him in my arms again.

"I knew you would come back and save me." He looked around not feeling safe out in the open. "Did you bring me some clothes?"

I smacked my forehead. "I'm so sorry. I forgot."

"Where is Beatrice?"

"I left her with Mrs. Holmes. We need to get you away from here."

"Who is Mrs. Holmes?"

Chapter 59

Nigel Crittenden

Search for the One-Armed Man

The day finally came that I was to be reassigned to a crossroads village called Ninety-Six. There was a small fortress there that was under constant harassment from the Rebels. It seemed to be some form of punishment to be banished to some obscure post away from all the activity along the coast. I nearly resigned my commission when I received word of my transfer. I couldn't. There was still unfinished business.

I decided to make one more walk along the battery which I had grown to appreciate during my time here. I would indulge myself with a stop at the Exchange dungeon for any word about Peter Smith. It was a pleasant morning. I was shocked at the ferocity of the storm the previous evening. There was debris littering the streets and gardens. Walking alone with my thoughts, I scanned the harbor and noted all the British ships. My chest always swelled with pride at the show of strength.

I turned onto Bay Street heading north. The breeze off the harbor picked up and nearly knocked me off my feet. Undeterred, I continued enjoying the morning air. Up ahead, I spied the outline of the large building that was my destination. Every fiber of my being told me that Smith was locked up there. I'm not sure why I expected the news to be different today. Maybe I just needed a little luck.

When I got to the building, I noticed there were just two guards at the entrance to the dungeon. There was some activity at the front of the building with red-coated officers going out in different directions. All the hustle and bustle of command. I turned to the guards. "I'm looking for a prisoner. Can you soldiers help me?"

The two men came to attention. One of them said, "No, sir. You would need to talk to Colonel Hampton. He is in charge."

I pursed my lips. "I'm just trying to see if a Rebel named Peter Smith is being housed here."

"We wouldn't know what their names are, Lieutenant."

"Have you seen a prisoner who is missing an arm?"

The guards glanced at each other.

"Well, speak up."

"Um, a man fitting that description was taken away this morning."

This was the best news I had heard in a long time, "Where was he taken?"

The soldier bit his lower lip. "Sir, he died and was carried away in a wagon for burial."

I instantly deflated. "Are you sure he died?"

They looked at each other again with troubled looks on their faces. "Yes, sir. He appeared to be dead."

"Where was he taken?"

One of the guards pointed up Bay Street. There is a place near the Cooper River where the prisoners are buried.

"How long ago?"

The guards looked like they would rather be anywhere other than here. "About an hour ago."

Maybe I could still catch up to the wagon to make sure that Smith was dead. I took long striding steps in the direction where the guard pointed. The city was coming to life and there was more activity on the streets. I passed both citizens and soldiers without as much of a glance. Then it hit me and I stopped and grabbed an elderly woman.

"Have you seen a wagon loaded with dead bodies pass by here?"

Her eyes were wide with fear. I released her and took a step back. "I'm sorry, ma'am. I meant no offense. I must find out about the bodies."

In a meek voice, she replied, "I am sorry, sir. I have not seen such a wagon."

Just as I turned to commence my pursuit, she added. "They usually bury the prisoners down that way." She pointed off in the direction where the Cooper River drains into the harbor. I tipped my hat and ran in the direction where she pointed. As I neared the river, I saw the wagon parked in a swampy area. There were two men dressed as common laborers working with shovels. "You men, are you burying prisoners from the Exchange building?"

They looked up at me and then glanced at each other.

"You have done nothing wrong. I am trying to find a prisoner who is missing his arm."

One of the men put down his shovel and took his hat in his hands. I watched while his fingers twiddled with the brim of the hat. "Sir, a man missing an arm was loaded into my wagon."

"Go on."

"Well, when I got here with Harry over there we started to unload the wagon and the body wasn't there."

I exploded. "What do you mean the body wasn't there?"

Both men were startled by my reaction. "It just wasn't there."

I tried to control my breathing. "Did anything happen on your way here?"

He put his hat back on his head and rubbed his chin. "There was this lady who stopped me. She was saying something about her missing child."

"Did you notice the one-armed man leave the wagon?"

"No, sir. The woman was quite agitated and I tried to calm her down."

"Which direction did she go?"

"I can't be sure, but that away." He pointed back toward the houses across from Bay Street. I looked around for any signs of the woman or Smith. It was an hour ago, they could be anywhere. I was so close and had all day to look for him.

Chapter 60

Peter Smith

Escaping Charleston

I limped after Anne as she led us through the back streets and alleys. My legs were betraying me and it was nearly impossible to keep up. I had trouble focusing and was delirious from lack of sleep and food. I seemed to be in a dream where sunlight was warming my face and I was with my wife. She darted her eyes at me and the ghastly look told me all I needed to know. She stopped at different points along the way to make sure we weren't being followed. It gave me a chance to catch my breath. I had to trust that Anne knew what she was doing.

We reached a corner and Anne made a motion with both hands, palms down and she turned the corner. I ducked down and waited. She returned a couple of minutes later and made the motion to follow her. We quietly crept past the line of row houses until we came to a modest home where Anne stopped. She smiled and started to climb the front steps. I timidly followed. She opened the door and went inside. I was closely behind her and when I entered I saw Beatrice in the arms of a woman I didn't know.

Anne took Beatrice in her arms. "Peter, this is Martha Holmes. We have been staying with her."

I nodded my head. "Mrs. Holmes, thank you for taking care of my family."

The corners of her mouth lifted up slightly, but I could see pain in her eyes. I turned my attention to my wife and child. I went to take Beatrice and she started to cry.

"Peter, she doesn't recognize you. You have lost so much weight. I will get you something to eat and you can rest."

When she and Beatrice left the room, Mrs. Holmes turned to me. "Is there any word about Jonathan?"

I suddenly remembered that Anne told me to find information about the man. I plopped down on a couch and tried to clear my mind. She continued to stare at me. I felt shame for not doing as I was told. "Where was your husband during the fight?"

She perked up a little. "He was in the trenches on the north side of the city."

I considered this. I didn't want to make it any worse for her. "I don't believe that he was in the dungeon with me. I heard some of the others say that most of the prisoners were placed on the British barges out in the harbor. I have no way to know if he is there or not." She stoically took the news and stood up. "Very well, let me get you some clean clothes to change into. You are about Jonathan's size."

I laid back and drifted off to a dreamless sleep.

I woke up some time later and found myself lying in bed. My filthy clothes had been stripped away and I felt cleaner. I reached up and rubbed my face, I was freshly shaved. How long had I been asleep? My head spun as I tried to sit up. I grabbed the side of the bed to steady myself. Standing slowly,

I shuffled over to the closed door. Just as I started to open it, Anne was standing on the other side. She leaned in and hugged me. "You're awake."

I released her hug. "How long have I been asleep?"

She let out a grunt. "It's been about twelve hours. Come let's get you some food."

I followed her down the stairs. Beatrice was playing on the floor. She looked up at me and smiled. I went to her and sat down next to her. "Beatrice, it's Daddy." She tilted her head and chuckled. My heart melted and I picked her up and held her tightly until she squealed to be released. I looked around at the modest possessions and entered the kitchen. Anne was placing some bread and cheese on the table. There is a smoldering pot of coffee. The smell was heavenly. I looked around. "Where is Mrs. Holmes?"

"She went out early this morning and has not returned."

I sat at the small table and started to stuff my mouth. Anne sat across from me watching. "We need to talk about what we are going to do."

I looked up from my meal and nodded my head.

"It's not safe to stay here. The British control everything."

I finished chewing on a piece of bread and took a sip of coffee. "They probably know that I am missing now. I'm not sure how interested they are in trying to find me, but I agree we need to leave."

She reached across the table and squeezed my hand. "The British are guarding the only road leaving the city. How do we escape?"

"We shall have to leave like I left Boston, by boat."

She looked unsure. "Where will we go?"

Good question. "Surely there are other members of the Army that made it out alive. We need to seek them out."

"There is something that I need to tell you."

I couldn't read her face whether it was good news or bad. "What is it?"

She smiled. "I am pregnant."

I sat back and gasped. "How far along?"

"I'm starting to show. Are you not happy?"

"I am, darling. The timing may not be the best."

Her face expressed her disappointment in my response. "That is all up to the good Lord, don't you think?"

I jumped when I heard the front door open. I started to get up and hide when Martha entered the kitchen. She had been crying and her eyes were red. She pulled out the chair next to Anne and collapsed. Anne was the first to speak. "What is it, Martha?"

"I asked around this morning. Mr. Smith is right about the prisoners being locked away on the barges. No one would tell me about Jonathan or if I could see him."

Anne reached over and put her hand on Martha's shoulder. "I'm so sorry. You can't give up hope."

Martha dabbed her eyes with a towel. "What am I to do now?"

Anne looked at me and I nodded. "Martha, we are going to leave Charleston. You are welcome to come with us."

She narrowed her glance. "How can I ever leave without Jonathan?" Anne removed her hand. "We understand."

"How are you going to leave Charleston? There are guards everywhere."

I spoke for the first time. "We will take a boat and go up the Cooper River until we are safe. Then we will try to join up with what's left of the Continental Army."

"Where are you going to get a boat?"

"We will steal one if we have to."

Martha took a deep breath. "I know someone who has a boat. I can ask them to take you."

Both Anne and I perked up. "Can you trust him?"

"The British have taken away his livelihood. He is no Tory. Let me talk to him and get it arranged."

Chapter 61

Nigel Crittenden

Frantic

I spent the rest of the day searching for any signs of Smith or the frantic woman. Everyone I stopped on the street denied seeing either the one-armed man or the woman. I stood in the middle of the roadway with my hands on my hips trying to think what I should do. My head spun as the world around me rotated. I couldn't find them by myself. I would need help. My orders dictated that I leave in the morning to report to my new post. Everything was spiraling out of control. This was the closest I had been to finding my enemy. Sometimes desperation requires making bold choices. I would go seek some help.

Dusk was descending as I made my way back to headquarters. I had to make General Clinton understand the importance of me staying long enough to find Smith and put this all to rest. I rehearsed what I would say to convince him of the urgency of my mission. I turned onto King Street and saw the two-story stately house where Clinton had his headquarters. Even at this time of day, a myriad of activity was going on. It reminded me of an ant hill that had been disturbed. I walked up to the gate which was guarded.

I was challenged when I tried to pass. One of the guards asked me the nature of my visit. This was too important for me to give up. In the strongest voice I could muster, "I need to see General Clinton about important business."

The guard rolled his eyes. "Wait here, Lieutenant...."

"Crittenden."

After a few tense minutes, I saw a major following the guard.

"What is the meaning of this Lieutenant?"

"Sir, it is important that I speak with General Clinton about a prisoner who escaped from the Exchange dungeon today."

He crossed his arms over his chest. "Why should the general be concerned over one prisoner?"

"This man isn't just another prisoner. He is a hero to the Rebel's cause. We should make every effort to recapture him."

The major titled his head. "What is this hero's name?"

I puffed out my chest. "Peter Smith."

"Never heard of him."

"He was a Naval officer whose ship destroyed HMS Progress...killing my father."

"I see. So this is for personal revenge then."

I hung my head. "Yes, sir. I suppose it is."

"Isn't there somewhere that you are to be right now Lieutenant? I will not bring this to the general's attention."

I didn't bother saluting the man. I turned away to go prepare myself to leave in the morning for Ninety-Six.

Chapter 62

Anne Smith

A Man Named Wilcox

I crept up to the bedroom door and cracked it open. I gasped when I saw Peter's face. He looked dead. I went to his side and could see him taking shallow breaths. I collapsed to the floor. It was almost more than I could bear seeing what he had gone through. Why couldn't he be content with all he did when we lived in Boston? There was no turning back now. We had to leave Charleston, but where would we go? I refused to be sent away again.

Martha returned later that morning. She had put on a strong face, but I had my doubts that she forgave Peter for not getting information about her husband. I stood up and waited while she removed the cotton wrap from around her shoulders.

"Were you able to talk to your friend?"

She brushed by me and went into the kitchen. I followed on her heels. I sensed danger. There was tension in the air thick enough to cut with a knife. Would her anger force her to turn Peter in to the British? She reached for a cup and poured water into it from a pitcher. She gulped the water with her back to me. Then she slowly turned and looked at me with no expression on her face. She sighed. "He told me that he would take you and your family out of Charleston on his boat. For a price."

One of my eyebrows lifted unconsciously. "What price?"

"Twenty pounds sterling silver."

I crumpled onto a chair. My eyes welled with tears. "Why such a large amount?"

For the first time, Martha's face softened. "There is great risk in taking you out of the city. There are British patrols everywhere."

"I need to talk to Peter. How soon does your friend need to know?"

"The sooner the better."

"Can we trust this man?"

"You don't have much choice."

My eyes drifted off as I thought about it. "You should come with us."

She shook her head. "I could never leave without finding Jonathan."

I still had reservations as I went to wake up Peter. I found him sitting up on the edge of the bed. "Are you well, husband?"

He turned toward the sound of my voice and smiled. "How long did I sleep?"

"A few hours. You need to regain your strength. We should stay here longer."

"You know it's not safe. Has Mrs. Holmes returned with news?"

I sat down next to him. "She has. Her friend agreed to take us for twenty pounds. In sterling silver."

"Do we have that much money?"

"We do, but it would not leave us with much."

He hung his head. "Maybe we can convince him to take less. How soon can we go?"

"The man told Martha the sooner the better."

—ele—

Two days later, we packed everything that we could carry on our backs and stole out of the boarding house before dawn. Martha saw us off. She fixed a breakfast of biscuits and small slices of ham. She even packed us some supplies for the road. I hugged her and wished her luck in finding Jonathan. We were directed to head north hugging the Cooper River until we got to the Gadson's wharf. We should look for a man holding a torch at the end of the pier. His name is Wilcox. Martha said that he was a fisherman.

It was a dark, moonless night. The streets were poorly lit which worked to our advantage and disadvantage. Peter carried Beatrice. He was still very weak and I kept an eye on him. We crept forward stopping at each intersection for any signs of British soldiers. The streets were eerily empty. On a couple of occasions we got lost and went in circles until we got our bearings. Martha told us that Wilcox would only wait until sunup. There was a sense of urgency to beat the rising sun.

When we got to the waterfront, we saw a line of British ships tied up. Their masts were silhouetted against the sky which started to turn an ashen color. We quietly picked up our pace. As we neared the end of a series of piers, I heard Peter whisper, "I need to put Beatrice down for a few minutes." We stopped and hid behind some crates to rest. I looked out to the eastern sky and felt panic rising in my chest. I turned to talk to Peter, then heard the sound of muffled voices coming from nearby. Then Beatrice let out a squeal. We froze. The voices went silent. We had no weapons to defend ourselves. We could only wait as Peter put his hand over Beatrice's mouth. The voices started up again and we heard the sound of boots walking on the wooden pier. When we were sure that it was safe to get moving, I grabbed Beatrice from Peter and took off. I didn't look back to make sure he was following. I now had a sense that we were running out of time.

We passed more piers and I heard the sound of the river sloshing up against the pilings. I squinted ahead against the darkness and saw the faint light of what looked like a lantern. I abandoned all caution and increased my pace. Behind me, I could hear the labored breaths of my husband. We reached a large wharf that had only a few boats tied up to it. This had to be the place. I raced down the wharf holding tightly onto my daughter. The sun's rays were breaking over the horizon. The lone figure started to move the lantern back and forth. I called out, "Mr. Wilcox?"

He hissed back, "Woman keep quiet. There are soldiers about."

I slowed down and felt the presence of Peter at my back.

"Are you the Smiths?"

"Yes, sir."

"Come on then, I was about to leave without you."

He helped us down a rickety wooden ladder to his boat. I climbed onto the wooden craft. It was only about fifteen feet long and didn't look very seaworthy. It had a small mast and sail and was rocking with the swells of the river. Once we were all abroad and settled, Wilcox untied the lines holding us to the dock and pushed away with an oar.

"Before we get very far I will need my payment."

Peter spoke up. "Twenty pounds is a steep price. Would you consider charging us less?"

Wilcox stood there with the oar in his hand. "Why would I do that?"

"Mrs. Holmes told us that you are a patriot. I am fighting for our common cause, trying to protect my family. Surely you can help us."

He stoically stood there rocking with the rhythm of the boat. I saw him look at Peter and his eyes scrolled down to the empty left sleeve. "Fifteen is the best I can do."

Peter reached into his pocket and pulled out a purse. He counted out the coins and handed them to the sailor. "Thank you, sir."

"I want all of you to lay down on the bottom of the boat and cover-up. It's getting light out and the redcoats will be watching."

We laid down as we were told and pulled a tarp over the top of us. I was concerned about Beatrice but she soon fell asleep. This was my first time on a boat. When I had time to realize where I was, my stomach started to churn and I feared that my breakfast biscuit would come back up. It didn't help that the surrounding marshes emitted a putrid odor adding to my discomfort. I lay afraid to move and prayed that we would make it safely across.

Chapter 63

Nigel Crittenden

Last Sightings

I spent a sleepless night thinking about my missed opportunity to capture Smith. I laid with my eyes wide open. At least I knew that he was in South Carolina. The question was where would he go, and would I get another chance to kill him? When the first signs of dawn came through the opening of my tent, I put my legs over the edge of the cot and sat up. We were getting an early start on our march inland. I yawned, stretched and reluctantly rose to prepare for the day. As I dressed, I heard the camp coming to life with the shouts of the sergeants rousing the men. There was comfort in the routine.

The men were being fed and the camp packed into waiting wagons as the sun broke over the horizon. The air was already thick and muggy. It would be another hot day. At least I was provided a horse to carry me on to my next duty station. We were camped within view of the Cooper River and the British warships tied up there. I stared out at the beauty of the area. The gentle river flowed out to the harbor which was surrounded by rings of small islands topped by palmetto trees. I wondered what the interior of the colony would behold.

Commencing the march, we were lined two men wide to accommodate the narrow streets. I rode near the head of the column with the other officers. My peers were engaged in a lively discussion on the virtues of Charleston. I maintained my silence as they argued about returning here after the war to live.

When we got to the intersection that would take us west away from the river, I took one last chance to gaze out over the majestic river. Something caught my attention and I had to shield my eyes against the rising sun which reflected across the top of the gently rushing water. It appeared to be a small vessel sailing in the middle of the river heading northeast. I guided my horse off the path to get a better view. The boat had a single mast and I could only make out a single figure aboard. Without taking my eyes off the boat, I reached down and pulled out my field glasses to get a better look. The distance was great and I couldn't focus to get a clear view. Just as I was about to give up and go back in line, there was movement. I sat up in the saddle and forced my eyes to get a better view. There was a tarp or piece of canvas that was moving. I swore that I saw a couple of heads pop up from under the covering. I clenched my fist and struck my leg. I couldn't tell if it was a man, woman or child. I twisted my head looking for assistance in stopping the vessel. From behind me, "Lieutenant, are you planning on joining us today?"

I blew out a breath of hot air. "Coming, Major." I returned to the formation. I took one more glance as we made our left turn to take us away from the city and off the peninsula. Maybe I was only imagining that there was someone else in that boat. The conversations continued as I had my doubts. Did Smith escape again?

We marched all day, going past the earthworks that were dug up by both sides during the siege. It had been weeks, but the unmistakable smell of battle and death lingered. I shook my head as there had been little effort to clean up the area. I supposed that was due to the Rebels being captured or run off. The remaining locals must not have had the desire to remove the remnants of their last stand. Would we have to destroy all the enemy cities to put down the rebellion? If so, there would be hundreds of years of hate here. Something akin to Ireland. I didn't understand why these people can't see the folly of their actions and return to being loyal citizens.

Once we broke out into open ground, there were small villages and farms with fields of cotton, corn and wheat. There was also a scattering of large plantations which were mostly abandoned by their owners. Left were hundreds of slaves who would come out and watch us march past. I was appalled at their condition. There were rumblings from the men and I detected their mood turned toward a hatred for anyone that would do this to another human being. We were given orders to offer freedom to any male slave who would join in the fight. We had a few takers, but most of these indentured souls looked like all joy had been taken from them. It was a sight that I shall never forget.

The march wasn't all a peaceful stroll through the park. The remnants of the Rebel Army took potshots at us as we passed. Especially in wooded areas where there was ample cover. It required us to send out soldiers to chase them away or kill them. This added delays to the march and we were already behind schedule. As we plunged deeper into the interior of the colony, stories were revealed about the hatred that the local citizens had for each other. Tales of murder and destruction of property all in the name of aligning as a loyalist or rebel were widespread. I saw the results myself with burned-out homes and dead bodies lying about. I noticed that this deeply affected the soldiers even though they had been hardened by the reality of war. There would be a reckoning one way or the other.

Chapter 64

Peter Smith

Finding Friends

I was still feeling the effects of my captivity as the small boat floated across the waves to our freedom. It was a comforting feeling to be on the water and I lay there under the tarp and considered how fortunate I was to be alive and reunited with my family. As I started to drift off to sleep, I felt a sudden movement and then Beatrice started to cry. I jerked my head to the side as Anne grappled with our daughter to calm her.

Mr. Wilcox hissed, "Keep that child silent. British soldiers are marching near the river!"

I sat up and poked my head out from under the covering. I scanned the shoreline and sucked in a mouthful of air. There was indeed a long line of redcoats. I stared intently at one man mounted on a horse and looking our way through a spyglass. Without thinking, I pulled the tarp back over my head and reached out to pull Anne and Beatrice back to the bottom of the boat. Anne protested. "Why did you do that, Peter?"

My mind raced. Could they be out looking for me? My brow furrowed. Surely they have no idea who I am. Why waste that many soldiers looking for me? I turned back to Anne. "I'm sorry, darling. I didn't want the British to see us." She looked uncertain as she held Beatrice tightly against her bosom.

We lay there in silence until we felt a sudden jolt from the boat ramming onto the shore. Wilcox whispered, "Keep your heads down while I make sure that it is safe." The boat rocked as he stepped out. Then the sensation of movement as he started to pull the boat on dry land. There was panic in Anne's eyes as we waited. A few minutes later, Wilcox said, "It's safe to come out." The tarp was lifted off of us and I had to shield my eyes against the brightness of the sun. Wilcox helped Anne and Beatrice onto the shore. I tried to stand up with weakened legs, struggling to make my way off the tiny vessel.

Wilcox pointed up the hill. "A horse and wagon are waiting for you. I advise that you take leave of this place. A word to the wise, keep to yourself. You never know who to trust these days."

I looked at the wagon and then back to him, my eyes questioning how he arranged for the ride. The corner of his mouth turned up and he winked. I tipped my hat and followed Anne up the hill. Reaching the summit, I bent over to catch my breath. Through my labored breathing, I heard, "Peter, what do we do now?" I stood up and put my arm on the dilapidated wagon. I twisted my head to scan for an avenue for our escape. We were surrounded by swamps that emitted a putrid odor. I spied a small dirt road cutting through the marshy low-lying land. "We need to listen to Mr. Wilcox and leave this area. I suppose returning to Boone Hall is out of the question. We need to find friends who can help us get away from the British. Looks like we only have one option." I pointed down at the ruts that had been cut into the ground.

She looked down to where I pointed and her eyes followed the so-called road until it disappeared into the treeline. She shrugged her shoulders and climbed onto the wagon with Beatrice. Thankful that we didn't have to walk, I climbed aboard and slapped the reins to get the horse moving. It was a jarring ride over the uneven lane. I didn't dare increase the pace of the horse over the terrain trying to prevent a broken leg. It was a welcome sight to reach the treeline. I knew we would be hidden from the view of the city. There was still danger here. Sweat ran down my back drenching my shirt as I tried to remain calm for Anne.

The further we got from the river the more the ground became stable. This made for a smoother ride. I was surprised by the lack of people and buildings. There was safety being hidden in the trees, but it blocked my view of which direction to take. I was somewhat familiar with the area. We were on Sullivan's Island and off to the east was Boone Hall. I had already decided against going there. I looked over at Anne and nodded. We would head north going inland. There was fear in her eyes, but she nodded back.

We slowly meandered through the woods for a couple of hours and came to an opening in the trees. There was a small stream, Hobcaw Creek, in front of us and on the other side there appeared to be a plantation. I stood up and looked around for signs of danger. There was activity on the grounds of the plantation, but no sign of redcoats. It was getting late in the afternoon and we were exhausted. I turned to Anne. "Should we chance it?" She stared at the large plantation house and turned to me with a hopeful look.

I took the reins tightly in my hand and took a deep breath. We eased forward into the rushing waters of the creek. The water was clear and I could see the rock-strewn bottom. It looked fordable, but we took it slowly. When we got halfway across, there was a shout from the other side that caught my attention. It was as if panic and pandemonium were breaking out. A number of the slaves started running from the fields, retreating to beyond the great house. We watched in shock as two men on horseback galloped in our direction. Anne reached over and grabbed my arm. I whispered under my breath, "Don't panic."

I continued to drive the wagon as the riders neared. As they got to the creek, one of the men yelled out, "What is your business here?" He was shabbily dressed with long blond hair and a stubbly growth of a beard on his gaunt face. He pulled down his slouch hat over his brow. I noticed that he was armed with a musket. I knew instantly that these men weren't the overseers from my time at Boone Hall. The other man trained his musket on us.

I replied, "We are looking for shelter. Is the owner available?"

They looked at us and around us. "Is there anyone else with you?"

"No, we are alone."

They talked among themselves and became animated. Anne and I looked at each other and I was about to turn the wagon around when we heard, "We will take you to Mrs. Reed. Follow us." I raised an eyebrow and did as I was told. Beatrice had been asleep through the drama. She awoke to the sounds of the men arguing and looked up at Anne. "Mama." Anne smiled and started rocking her.

We reached the other side of the creek and went up an embankment on a path that led to the plantation home. The slaves slowly came out of their hiding places and stared at us. It made me wonder what had happened here. When we got to the entrance of the mansion, one of the men said, "Wait here."

We watched him climb the stairs and knock on the door. He was admitted inside and we waited. A few minutes later, the man exited followed by an elegantly dressed woman. She looked to be in distress with her golden hair amiss and dark circles under her eyes. Her head jerked in rapid movements looking around. She came down to the wagon. "What can I do for you?"

I sensed danger and my skin began to crawl. What if she was a Tory? I squeezed my eyes shut and prayed for the best. "Ma'am, we are fugitives from the British in Charleston and I was hoping you could assist my wife, daughter and me."

She tilted her head. "Are the British chasing you right now?"

"I don't believe they are."

She stood there and seemed to consider my response. "I can't be too careful about who I allow on my property. There was a raiding party that came through here taking supplies and trying to get my slaves to join them. My husband is up north serving with General Washington. I am left to run this place by myself. Why don't you come into the house and I can get you a meal and we can talk."

As we climbed down from the wagon, she turned to one of the men. "Mr. Andrews, please take care of their horse and wagon."

"Yes, Mrs. Reed."

We followed her up the stairs and into the house. We stood in the parlor and I looked around amazed at the obvious display of wealth. Mrs. Reed noticed my expression. "This home has been in my family for generations. It's all we can do to keep it running now." She noticed Beatrice and smiled. "Where are my manners? Please make yourself comfortable while I go get the servants to put together a meal."

We watched her leave the room and took a seat on a couch. Anne put Beatrice on the floor so she could run around. "How safe are we here, Peter?" I shrugged my shoulders. "She said her husband was in the Army. We should be fine. The quicker we leave the better." The lady of the house returned a few minutes later. "If you would please follow me into the dining room." We were seated at a large rectangle-shaped table. There were plates of dried meat and cooked vegetables on the table. The smell was heavenly. It had been awhile since we last ate and we plunged into our meal. Mrs. Reed watched us eat.

"I'm sorry I can't offer you more. The British left us with little."

I wiped my mouth with a napkin. "This is wonderful, Mrs. Reed. If I may ask a question?" She nodded. "Why didn't the British burn down everything?"

She sat back pondering the question. "Well, Mr...." "Smith, ma'am. Peter Smith. This is my wife Anne Smith."

"Mr. Smith, I also considered that. The officer in charge, Colonel Tarleton, was ruthless in his actions but decided to spare my home. It didn't stop him from taking my stores of food and some of my most able field servants."

I did my best not to react to that last statement. "Did he know about your husband?"

"I believe he did. I just thank my blessings that he spared me." She folded her hands on the table and leaned toward me. "Now let me ask you a question, Mr. Smith. Why are you and your family fugitives?"

I sat back and rubbed my stomach. "I am an officer in the American Army. I was stationed at Fort Moultrie during the British invasion. When General Lincoln surrendered to the British, I was taken captive and locked up in Charleston. I never thought I would escape until Anne came and saved me." I reached over and grabbed Anne's hand.

"Is that how you lost your arm?"

I looked down at the table. "No, I lost it in a naval battle earlier in the war."

She had a shocked look on her face. "Then why are you still fighting?"

I looked up with resolve in my eyes. "Because we have not gained our independence yet."

Mrs. Reed provided us with a bed to sleep in. In the morning after a small breakfast, we were back on the road heading north.

Chapter 65

Nigel Crittenden

Star Fort

O ur small company of men and officers reached the outpost at Nine-ty-Six two days later. I still couldn't shake the feeling that I let Smith escape again. I tried to convince myself I was being irrational and the man could be anywhere. More than likely he was still in Charleston or dead. Once we were settled in and camped among the other troops posted at the small fort, I reached out to the commanding officer. I introduced myself to Lieutenant Colonel John Cruger. He was strolling around the camp when I caught up to him. "Colonel, Lieutenant Crittenden reporting for duty."

He sized me up with piercing slate colored eyes. "Welcome, Lieutenant. We certainly could use your men to defend against these incessant attacks by the rebels. Let me give you the tour." He started to walk off and I joined him. We walked to the perimeter which had been cleared of trees for open fields of fire to avoid any sneak attacks by the Rebels. There was a creek that ran nearby and provided water for the camp. He turned and walked back to the fort. "The place is called Star Fort due to its shape. As you can see the top is lined with trees that we cut down and it is surrounded by a ditch in which we have placed sharpened limbs for added protection." He led me into the fort itself. "The structure is large enough to accommodate the five hundred men in the garrison. We have three, three-pound cannons for added defense."

I stood at the top of the palisade and scanned out in all directions. "Very impressive, sir. How often have the enemy tried to attack?"

He stood there looking out and let out a loud chuckle. "The riff-raff have made several disconcerted efforts to dislodge us from here. It is nothing more than an inconvenience. We must maintain control of this area as the other forts in the vicinity are supplied through the roads that go through here." He pointed out the dirt paths emanating from the fort.

"If you don't mind me asking. Sir....."

"What's on your mind, Crittenden?"

"You and your men don't appear to be part of the regular Army."

I could see by the hurt look on his face that I had touched a raw nerve.

"My men and I are just as loyal to the King as you are. We are proud to be here in the fight against these rebels who would try to change our way of life. We have men here from New York, New Jersey and South Carolina."

I bowed. "I meant no disrespect."

My apology seemed to placate him. "As I said, I welcome you and your men. I suspect that the attacks will continue and we need to be prepared for whatever they throw at us."

Over the next few weeks, I led patrols out into the surrounding area to search for any Rebel activity. Since we captured Charleston, there had been a noticeable decline in signs of any semblance of an army. It was as if they had melted into the surrounding hills. We encountered random potshots from hidden men in the woods that never amounted to much. It gave the men something to do to try and track down the offenders.

As I rode at the head of the column of men heading back to the fort, I started to question why I was in America again. Over the few years, since I came to this place, I had been involved in only three major engagements. The rest of my time was spent on guard duty. It was hardly a record to be proud of. Added to this was my complete and utter failure to avenge my father. Self-doubt crept into my soul again. I was homesick for my mother and home.

We rounded the corner that took us out of the trees into the opening where the fort was placed. I was jolted out of my trance by the rapid sound of gunfire. This was no minor raid. I turned to my trusty Sergeant. "Clarke, it appears that we are needed. Get the men in line to attack the enemy. I will ride ahead to see what we are facing." I set my horse to a gallop. There was a blanket of smoke covering the field as both sides were firing at each other. There was also the unmistakable sound of cannon fire from the fort. The sulfur-smelling smoke made it hard to see what was happening. I entered the fort from the rear to search out Colonel Cruger. I spied him atop the rampart directing fire on the attackers.

He took notice of me and yelled out, "Crittenden, so glad you could join us. The rebels are making a serious attempt to dislodge us. There must be a few hundred men out there." He looked around behind me. "Where are your men?"

I directed them to attack the enemy's flank and drive them back."

He stared off in the direction I was looking. "Well done, Lieutenant. That should give them pause for their attack." He turned his attention back to the business at hand. I ran to the other side of the fort to see how my men were faring in their attack. I pulled out my spyglass and tried to see through the haze of smoke. I made out the outline of my red-coated company forcing their way into the woods. The gunfire was hot and I could see my men were taking casualties while driving the Rebels back. I clenched my fist while letting out a yell. I should be down there. I ran down the rampart back to my horse and rode to join them.

I caught up with my men to join in the battle. The fighting raged on for another hour. The Rebels made repeated attempts to storm the fort. Each time they were repelled taking heavy casualties. The gunfire began to ebb and the Rebels retreated into the trees leaving dozens of their dead and dying on the field. I rode among my men. They were in high spirits over another victory over the Americans. I was dismayed by the report from Sergeant Clarke concerning our losses. My choice to attack the Rebel flank was a sound decision but at a high cost. As the men were tended to, I wondered what this attack meant. Were the Americans trying to assert themselves by taking the battle back at us?

Chapter 66

Anne Smith

Cabin in the Woods

As we rode away from the plantation, I was hopeful that Peter had enough fighting. He had nearly died in that prison and I saw signs of the toll that it took. I had to convince him to go home. I missed my parents terribly. They were missing seeing Beatrice grow and now with the new baby that they didn't know about, it was hard to sit here and not say anything. I waited until I was about to burst. "Peter, we need to talk."

He turned to me. "What is it, dear?"

I took a deep breath and blurted out. "I think that we need to go home to Boston."

He hung his head. "What would you think of me if I abandoned my duty?"

"I would think that you did your part and now it's time to take care of your family. Don't you miss your parents? You also have to consider our unborn child."

He slowly lifted his head. I was shocked to see tears in his eyes. Then as he began to sob, I pulled his head onto my bosom. Beatrice began to cry at the sight of her father in distress. My heart melted and I cried. After we had all gained control, Peter mumbled. "I think you are right. It's time to go home."

"Oh, Peter, do you mean it?"

He nodded his head and tried to smile, but I could see the pain on his face.

"What do we do now?"

He pulled back on the reins to stop the horse. "We have little money and we are in the middle of a British-controlled area. We have to find friends that can help us."

"Where do we go?"

"I'm not sure. There have to be like-minded patriots somewhere nearby." He slapped the reins and the horse trudged forward down the tree-lined path. "Maybe you should pray that we find the right person somewhere on this road."

We rode in silence for a few hours until we came to a small village. The first sight that we saw was a smoldering building on the edge of town. It looked like a home that had been burnt down to the foundation. The acrid smell of smoke could still be detected. I looked around for any signs of danger. No British soldiers in sight. We continued to ride into town. There were a few people on the main road, mostly women and the elderly. We came across an old man who was stooped over. Peter asked, "Excuse me, sir. What town is this?"

He stared at me with untrusting eyes. "Who's asking?"

"We are just passing through and trying to get our bearings."

He noticed me and Beatrice. "This isn't a safe place for your family right now. You are in Moncks Corner."

"What happened?"

He followed Peter's gaze to the destroyed home. "British cavalry came through yesterday looking for Rebels. That would be the mayor's house. He didn't want to cooperate with that crazy British officer."

"Did they hurt anyone?" Peter looked around. "Any other damage?"

The old man shook his head. "Not sure what happened to the mayor. They rode on after burning down the house. What is your business here?"

Peter looked at me and I emphatically shook my head no. He went ahead anyway. "We are fugitives from Charleston and looking for safe passage north."

The old man rubbed his stubble-covered chin. "That would make you a Rebel."

I grabbed Beatrice waiting for the old man to sound the alarm. Instead, his lined face broke into a devious smile. "Heard tell that what's left of the Army is in Camden. You should find what you're looking for there. It's about one hundred miles that away." He pointed off to the north. "Word of warning, stay clear of that British cavalry officer name of Tarleton. He has evil in his eyes."

I shuddered as Peter started to drive the wagon off to the north.

All along the way, we saw more signs of damage. Burnt structures lined the road. At one of the destroyed homes, three bodies were laying out in a row, like they had been posed. I gasped at the sight which stirred Beatrice from her nap. She started to climb up in the back of the wagon. Peter hissed, "Don't let her see that." I pulled her into my arms and held her against me. She started to struggle as I turned to my husband. "Has the war come to this? Why are they killing women and children?"

His eyes were ablaze with hatred. "Emotions get out of control and even the innocent are made to pay." Under my breath, I whispered, "I can't wait to leave this place."

We stopped under the shadow of a large elm tree to eat a meal of the provisions we were given at the plantation. I chewed on a hard biscuit and watched Beatrice walk timidly across knee-high grass in a meadow. Out of the corner of my eye, I watched Peter wince as he tried to move his shoulder. He told me that there were times when he could still feel his missing arm. I put the biscuit down and whipped the crumbs from my fingers. "Peter, we need to find someplace to sleep for the night. All three of us are exhausted."

He continued to chew on a piece of dried beef and looked around. "Of course you're right. I'm concerned about the British cavalry roaming these woods. I don't know if I would be able to talk our way out of any trouble." He stood up and started to walk down the path swiveling his head from side to side.

I took a quick look at Beatrice and started following him. "What are you looking for?"

Without turning, he said, "I'm trying to see if there are any abandoned structures in the woods for us to stay for the night."

I turned to check on Beatrice who had come onto the road to follow. When I turned back, Peter was nowhere to be seen. "Peter, where are you?"

"I'm down here."

I waited until Beatrice caught up, grabbed her hand and followed his voice. There was a wheel-rutted path that was overgrown with weeds. It snaked into the woods. The birds cried out in protest as we slowly stepped over the uneven ground. We came to an opening and Beatrice cried, "Dada." He was standing in front of an ancient abandoned shack. The roof had partially collapsed and there were holes in the stone walls.

Peter turned at the sound of Beatrice's voice. "This should do. We will be secluded, safe from the British."

"Are you sure it's safe to stay here?"

"It looks better on the inside. I will go get the wagon. Why don't you start a fire in the fireplace?"

I stood there open-mouthed as he raced off. I cautiously peeked into the cabin. It was mostly intact with a usable fireplace. I was overcome by a musty smell. The dirt floor was littered with garbage. In the corner, there were remnants of a bed covered in tattered blankets. I picked up the blanket and jumped as a nest of mice went scurrying in every direction. After allowing myself to calm down, I went outside with Beatrice to collect sticks to make a fire. Peter returned with the wagon and helped us gather firewood. We got a blazing fire started just as the sun dipped below the trees and the area was masked in darkness. The air had cooled off from the summer heat by a gentle breeze. The warmth from the fire felt good. We stayed in that cabin for two days.

Chapter 67

Nigel Crittenden

Letters From Home

There was an eerie silence. Even the birds had deserted us. I stared up at the night sky where I could see an endless number of stars displayed across a cloudless sky. It was times like this when I enjoyed this country. The heat had begun to dissipate with the setting sun. A gentle breeze moved the thick air and the smell of cooking meat permeated. It had been two weeks since the Rebels had attacked in force. Life went back to the drudgery of garrison duty. We were still guarding the supply trains that passed through and even fought off small bands of Rebels. Still, it seems that I was thousands of miles from the real war.

There was talk around camp about the string of victories over the Americans since General Cornwallis took command of the Army in the southern colonies. After the success of capturing Savannah and Charleston, came the stunning defeat of a superior force of colonists at the Battle of Camden. It was said that the remnants of the embarrassed traitors fled north into North Carolina leaving South Carolina free of Rebels. I knew better based on the most recent attack here. I wondered how much longer could they hold out.

A packet of letters arrived in camp causing a stir and lifting the spirits of everyone. I received five letters from my mother. It took months for them to catch up with me. I sat in my tent and my hands trembled as I began reading them. She conveyed her concern over my well-being in each letter. She wanted Justice for my father, but was strongly against me coming here. As the wife of a naval officer, she understood the life and the calling. She reasoned that losing my father to this war was enough for our family. I slumped in my chair and the letters fell to the ground as I remembered our exchange on the day I left. I had returned home after completing my schooling and was giving her the news of my assignment to America. She sat stoically as I recited my orders with pride in my voice. After I completed reading her the orders, she said, "You will get yourself killed like your father." I felt ashamed and like she slapped me with her words. "Mother, it is exactly why I am going to avenge my father." She brushed a hand at me. "It won't bring him back."

The thought of her words still bothered me. What started as my life's mission to avenge my father had turned into years of going from battle to battle and not finding Smith. The joy I should have felt to hear from my mother turned into a soul-wrenching melancholy for my failings. I had almost convinced myself to give up searching for Peter Smith. Now, reading these letters from my mother gave me an added incentive to complete my task. I would show her that I was as good a man as my father.

The next day I marched into Lieutenant Colonel Harris's tent. I pushed past the guard standing at the entrance. Harris looked up from his desk. "What is the meaning of this intrusion, Crittenden?"

"Sir, I respectfully request transfer to a command that is actively seeking out the Rebels to end this war."

Harris sat back and smiled. "I like your exuberance young man, but not your insolence." He shuffled through the paperwork in front of him. "As chance would have it, there is correspondence from General Cornwallis requesting available men for an upcoming offensive to clear the Carolinas completely of Rebels. Would that be to your liking, Lieutenant?"

I stood at attention. "Yes, sir. How soon can I leave?"

The older man smirked. "I will submit your name, then we wait to hear back from General Cornwallis."

"Thank you, sir." I left the tent and doubled over nearly vomiting.

It took three weeks to receive my orders. I was to report to Lieutenant Colonel Banestre Tarelton. The orders indicated that he would be found somewhere in the vicinity of Laurens County. The document indicated that the Colonel and his men are usually on the move. I packed my belongings and was on the road the following morning.

Chapter 68

Peter Smith

Disaster at Camden

I woke up to the sound of a loud crash. I tried to remember where I was. I propped myself up on my elbow and strained to see anything in the predawn light. I tilted my head to listen for any other signs of movement. Nothing. I looked down and saw that Anne and Beatrice were still asleep. I was more exhausted than I would admit and it was the right choice to stay in this dilapidated cabin. I shivered from a chill in the air and noticed that the fire had burnt down to embers.

I quietly got up and looked out the door of the cabin. No signs of anything that could have made that noise. Maybe an animal. I sucked in a breath of air and rushed behind the cabin. Our horse was grazing in the long grass and the wagon was still parked where I put it. I stroked the mane of the horse and thought to myself. We are almost out of supplies, I don't have a weapon to defend us or to hunt, and we only have a small amount of money. A madman was roaming the area looking for supporters of the rebellion. Our choices were slim. Continue until we run into someone who can assist us in escaping north, or turn myself in so that my family can survive. I rubbed my chin, not much of a choice.

I felt a presence behind me and tensed up. "Peter, what are you doing out here?"

I turned to see Anne with a concerned look and rubbing her sides with her arms. "I heard a noise and was checking to make sure the horse was safe."

She came to me and put her arms around my waist. Her touch felt so good. "We must get back on the road this morning. I fear that we won't have enough supplies to last much longer."

She nodded. "I'll get Beatrice up and we can go."

I said a prayer while I hitched up the horse. "Lord, please look after my family and protect us on our travels. Amen."

We continued to see damage to farms and houses the closer we got to Camden. No more dead bodies, which was a blessing. Even though it was late September, the heat was oppressive during the day. The trees provided some relief, but we endured the hot and muggy conditions in the slow-moving wagon. From the back of the wagon, a little voice piped up. "Mama, I hungry." Anne looked at me as if prodding me to do something. "We will find something to eat, Beatrice." I looked at Anne for support. She picked her up. "That's right, dear. We shall stop and eat very soon."

I started to diligently look for a safe place to stop. I would resort to stealing food if we became desperate. After another couple of miles, we came upon a lone house that was off the main road. From our vantage point, it appeared deserted. I raised my eyebrows at Anne and turned the horse toward the house. When we got closer, the door swung open and a woman stood at the stoop holding a rifle. Her hair was hanging in her face and she wore a worn dress. Behind her stood two small children. There was fire in her eyes. She pointed the weapon in our direction. "What do you want?"

I held up my lone arm. "We are unarmed and seeking assistance, ma'am. No reason to point your musket at us."

She didn't seem to be convinced and cocked the rifle. "What kind of assistance?"

I keep my arm up. "We need to feed our daughter and are looking for news about the location of the Continental Army."

She shifted her eyes to Beatrice in Anne's lap and lowered the gun. "Get down off your wagon slowly and keep your arms where I can see them." As I climbed down, she called out. "What happened to your other arm?"

I jumped off the wagon and started to walk her way. "I lost it fighting against the British."

She lowered the rifle until the tip touched the ground. She wiped her brow with her hand. "Come in the house. Let me see what I can get you to eat."

We followed her into the modest home. It was a small, crowded, three-room dwelling. I saw the fields behind where dead stalks of corn stood like sentries. There weren't any slaves. These people were poor farmers. The woman was rummaging in her pantry and pulled out some bread and cheese. She placed them on the table and collapsed into a chair. Her children, a boy and a girl, stood behind her watching us. Anne carried Beatrice over to the table and started to tear at the bread and cheese, stuffing it in her mouth while giving some to our daughter. I gingerly walked over to a chair near the lady of the house and sat down.

"Where is your husband?"

She looked at me with dull eyes that had lost their fire. "He ran off to fight the British and I haven't seen him since. He left me here alone to raise the children and tend to the farm."

"Are there any American soldiers in the area?"

She tilted her head. "Haven't you heard about the disaster at Camden?"

"I was in a prison in Charleston and have not heard anything."

She leaned toward me. "Well, the British scattered the whole bunch off to North Carolina. Those are the ones that didn't get killed or captured."

"Is that where your husband is?"

She shrugged her shoulders.

I sat back in the chair and looked over at Anne who was still stuffing her mouth. "Have you seen any British cavalry riding through here recently?"

"They passed through about a week ago. I heard they were doing terrible things to innocent people."

"Is all hope lost?" I said mostly to myself.

The woman touched my hand. "I heard from someone in town that General Washington sent General Greene to South Carolina to take the state back. I haven't seen any of those soldiers."

"General Greene. You mean Nathanael Greene?"

"I suppose that's him."

"I know General Greene."

I stood up. "Do you have any idea where the general might be?"

She tried to think and looked bewildered. "Maybe in the upstate."

"How far is that from here?"

"Maybe a hundred miles."

I turned to Anne. "We need to find General Greene. He will be able to help us. Ma'am, thank you for your hospitality and information. Can you spare any more food and maybe a weapon?"

She stood up and started for the kitchen. "Caleb, go grab your Pa's other rifle." The boy dutifully went into the bedroom. She grabbed a sack and started stuffing in bread, corn and some potatoes. This is all I can spare."

The boy came back and handed me an ancient looking flintlock along with a powder horn and some musket balls.

I grabbed a piece of bread off the table and stuffed it in my mouth. We walked out the door and Anne reached out and hugged the woman. When we got to the wagon, she said, "Do you think her husband ran off?"

"I think he is either dead or a prisoner which is just as bad."

We continued north. This time to find Nathanael Greene.

Chapter 69

Nigel Crittenden

Chasing Tarleton

I was assigned a squad of men to accompany me to find Colonel Tarleton. There was danger in this part of the colony where an attack could come at any time. We were diligent as we marched through the heavily wooded areas where snipers could hide without being detected. Since the summer heat had given way to autumn, the leaves on the trees had started their annual death fall from the trees. This provided us with somewhat better visibility, but I could not bring myself to relax.

I was given vague instructions as to where I could find the colonel. We headed in a generally northwest direction. After a while, it became evident that we were on the right path by the appearance of burnt down homes and barns. I heard tales of the ruthlessness of Tarleton. He was a favorite of command due to the results he delivered. I wondered about that. His actions would stir generational hate against us. Even if we won this war, the fighting would never end.

As we entered a small village in an opening in the woods, the citizens could be seen scattering away from the road. I halted the squad and watched the spectacle. Something told me we were on the right path. I ordered the men to stay behind and I rode into the town. I saw an old man smoking a pipe. He was sitting on a rocking chair. I rode up to him. He had a scowl on his face and his gray eyes remained locked on me. When I got close he stopped rocking. His hate was noticeable.

"Excuse me, sir. Have you seen any cavalry come through here commanded by a man named Tarleton?"

He removed the pipe from his mouth without taking his eyes off me. "Mayhaps I did. They came tearing through here about four hours ago. They stopped long enough to question everyone about seeing any rebels. They threatened to burn down the town if we didn't tell them what they wanted to hear."

"What happened?"

He puffed out some air. "We didn't know of any and told them that. That Tarleton fella was angry and he was snapping out orders to burn the town. Then for some reason, he changed his mind and the whole lot of them rode off."

"Which direction did he go?"

The old man pointed his pipe down the road that led west out of town.

I looked in that direction. "Did they say where they were going?"

He shook his head and put the pipe back in his mouth. I tipped my hat and rode back to the column of men under my command. "Men, we are about four hours behind Colonel Tarleton. We will continue to march west for the rest of the day." When we reached the town, some of the locals lined the street to watch us. The old man must have told them we were harmless.

One of the men called out. "What town is this?"

A woman answered, "Laurensville."

We continued to seek out Tarleton and his men. They seemed to be just out of reach. While Laurensville had been left unscathed, we entered another village that wasn't as fortunate. A plume of smoke could be seen before we entered the town. The flames were still engulfing the structure and several bodies were lying in the yard. The townspeople were too distracted fighting the blaze to notice us. I turned and ordered the men to fall out and assist in dousing the flames. I dismounted my horse to supervise when an elderly woman spotted me and charged in my direction. She had a full head of steam and I saw hate in her eyes.

"Why are you here? You can see what your kind has already done." She came up right in my face and I took a step back.

"Madam, I assure you that we are not here to harm anyone. Who did this?"

She bent over and put her hands on her knees. I felt for her and wanted to console her, but thought better of it. After a couple of minutes, she straightened up. "It was some of your kind. They came here looking for rebels." She pointed to the burning house. "They found three deserters hiding in that house and brought them outside. Shot them where they stood. Then that monster ordered the house to be burnt."

I didn't have to ask who she was talking about. "How long ago were they here?"

"About two hours or so."

I put my hands on my hips. "How many soldiers were here?"

She thought about it for a few seconds. "There were a couple dozen soldiers on horse and maybe one hundred others."

I looked back and noticed that the fire was mostly under control. The air was still thick with black smoke and the sun was starting to set. We were only a few hours behind Tarleton. I hoped that they would camp for the night. I decided to get my men out of this town and camp on the other side away from these poor people. I went about organizing the men. I looked back as the citizens stood and watched us march away. I wondered what they were thinking.

Chapter 70

Anne Smith

The Scout

I felt the baby kick. I looked over at Peter and almost told him. He was deep in thought. All this traveling couldn't be good for the baby or Beatrice. The rocking of the wagon over the uneven roadway made me nauseous. I trusted my husband, but how much longer would this go on? It was getting colder being trapped in the middle of towering oak trees. I wrapped my shawl tightly around my shoulders and looked down at my sleeping daughter. Would she remember any of this? We need to be someplace safe away from all this misery.

We had been on the road for a couple of days since leaving the small farm near Camden. I kept expecting to run into the British Army that was destroying homes. So far we had been spared that misery. About mid-day we entered into a small community that had a dozen small homes and a few scattered businesses. The steeple of a small church was located in the middle of the village. We were nearing the end of the year and there was a hint of snow in the air. We pulled into town and there was some activity by the locals. They did not seem to be concerned about our arrival.

Peter pulled in front of a tavern that advertised rooms to let. He looked at me and I emphatically shook my head up and down. He climbed down and went inside. I gathered Beatrice and a bag we kept our clothes in. After a few minutes, Peter returned with a smile. "They can accommodate us. It's warm inside. They are serving stew. I asked what town this was. The proprietor told me this is Chester."

"Are we safe here?"

He shrugged his shoulders. We went inside and my eyes had to adjust to the dimly lit room. There was a roaring fire in the corner. There was a scattering of tables that were occupied by a few men. The two windows on the outer wall were coated with grim and didn't allow any light to shine through. Peter grabbed Beatrice and I followed him to a staircase that led to the upper level. Our room was modestly equipped with a bed and dresser with a wash basin on top. It was drafty but it would do.

"Let's go get some stew."

I nodded to Peter. "Let me wash up some, you and Beatrice go ahead." After the door closed, I undressed and tried to wash days of dirt and dust off me. I dressed feeling refreshed for the first time in weeks. When I got downstairs, Peter was engaged in a discussion with a man I had not noticed earlier. "Peter, who is your friend?"

Both men turned at the sound of my voice. "Anne, this is Jonathan Taylor. Mr. Taylor, my wife Anne." The gentleman stood up and bowed his head. "Mrs. Smith."

Peter looked around. "Anne, Mr. Taylor is a patriot. He is scouting ahead for General Greene." I got a better look at the man. He was shabbily dressed with long stringing hair and a long flowing beard. I rolled my eyes at Peter. He mouthed, "He's safe." I had a feeling of dread. Beatrice let out a chirp. She was sitting on Peter's lap eating some bread. I sat down and a bowl of steaming stew was placed in front of me. My mouth started to water at the rich smell.

The two men continued their conversation while I ate my dinner. They spoke in muffled tones but I picked up some of what they were saying. Something about the location of General Greene's Army somewhere on the border between North Carolina and South Carolina. Peter had that look in his eyes. I began to doubt that we would go home to Cambridge.

I woke up when the sun's rays seeped through the window and crept over my face. I had the best night's sleep in as long as I could remember. I reached over for Peter. He was gone. I sat up and searched the room. Beatrice was sleeping on a blanket on the floor. No sign of Peter. I started to panic. Was this something to do with that man Peter was talking to last night? I slipped out of the covers and started dressing when the door opened. Peter came in with a tray of food and coffee.

"Where have you been?"

He looked offended by my angry outburst.

"I was getting breakfast." He sat the tray on the bed and handed me a mug of coffee. He watched me sip at my cup. I knew him well enough that he wanted to talk to me about something.

"What is it, Peter?"

He cleared his throat and fidgeted with the tray. "Mr. Taylor can take me to see General Greene." I waited for more. He didn't make eye contact. "I have paid for the room for a week, including meals. I want you and Beatrice to stay here while I'm gone."

I could feel my blood start to boil. "Peter, you promised that we could go home."

"I know. I still have unfinished work to do. I need you to understand this is something I have to do."

I slammed the mug down on the tray spilling its contents on the bed. "I'm tired of that same old excuse! You won't stop until you're dead."

He tried to hug me. I pushed him away. He bent down and picked up Beatrice who had started to stir. "Little one, Daddy needs to leave for a while. I will be back." He then grabbed his belongings and the rifle he was given and went to the door.

I crossed my arms over my chest. "I may not be here if you come back." He paused, then opened the door and was gone.

Chapter 71

Peter Smith

Back in Action

I didn't look back at Anne when I left. I know that I made a promise to go home, but there was some magical force that drew me to conflict. Maybe it's from the abuse I endured as a child or the exhilaration that I felt each time I'm under pressure in a life-or-death situation. She would eventually forgive me. I have to do this. It might be the last time I can make a difference.

Mr. Taylor was waiting for me. He had a determined look on his face. "I have two horses out back. We need to stay off the main roads. There are British units everywhere. I'll take you to Greene's camp. The rest is up to you. I need to report my findings to him anyway."

We mounted in the early morning light and bundled up against the crisp chill in the air. I was trusting everything to this man, who I just recently met. Deep down, I wanted to believe he was who he said he was. I shall find out soon enough.

We rode steadily north avoiding cities and main roads. We crossed small creeks in back country areas where there were no roads or trails. On one harrowing occasion, we came across a British patrol made up of twelve horsemen. We barely made it into a dense thicket of shrubs and hardwoods. The patrol didn't seem to be in a hurry and was leisurely trotting down the narrow lane that acted as a road. The arrogant look on their faces told the story that they believed they had won the war. It made my blood boil and emboldened me even more.

The patrol was heading south and we waited a few minutes to make sure they were out of sight before continuing. I didn't know much about my guide. He stared ahead and wasn't very talkative. "Mr. Taylor, how did you get involved in all this?"

He turned my way. "You can call me Jonathan. I'm from Virginia originally. I fought the French under George Washington as part of a colonial militia unit under the British. I was an officer in the militia. I was loyal to the King and believed in what I was doing. That all changed by the way we were treated by the British regulars. They considered us to be a lower class and not to be trusted. Washington was a great leader, even though he was disrespected. After the war, I drifted around until you men up in Boston started raising a ruckus." He smiled at me. "Anyway, I felt like I needed to get involved and looked up my old commander for a job. He knew of my special skills and recruited me to do this business."

My mouth hung open. "You know General Washington?" He nodded. "I met the man, but only briefly. I was instantly drawn to him."

He chuckled. "He has a way of doing that."

"Aren't you concerned about what the British will do to you if they capture you?"

"I'm a cautious man by nature. In saying that, I understand the risk and am willing to pay the price if need be."

We rode the rest of the day in silence.

Around noon of the next day, we came to the outskirts of the sleepy little village of York. At least that's what Jonathan said. I had no idea where we were. We remained hidden as he tried to see if there was any activity. He squinted trying to get a better view. He let out a growl and hissed, "Stay here. I'm going to get closer to see who is in that town." He didn't wait for me to respond and started crawling toward the village.

I followed him with my eyes until he was out of sight. The horses started to whine behind me as if spooked. Before I could turn my head, I heard, "Well, look what we got here. Must be a British spy."

I froze embarrassed that I allowed them to sneak up on me.

"Why don't you be a good lad and stand up slowly."

I turned in their direction as I struggled to get to my feet. Two Continental soldiers had their muskets trained on me.

"Look men, you have it all wrong. I am an officer in the regular Army. I was captured in Charleston, but I was able to escape. I am looking for General Greene."

"Did you hear that Randall, the one-armed man, is an officer?" Randall laughed.

"You men take me to the General. He knows who I am."

"Who are you?"

"I am Colonel Peter Smith from Boston."

Both of them laughed at that. The first soldier twisted his head at the sound of the horses whining again. "Well, well, two horses. Where is your friend...Colonel...?"

"He went into town to make sure the British weren't there."

"We will escort you into town, but if no one knows you we'll have to hang you as a spy." Randall prodded me with his musket and I started walking down the road. I started sweating as I walked considering my predicament. I didn't have any identification on me. What if General Greene wasn't there to vouch for me? Where did Taylor go?

We got to the outskirts of the town. The citizens stopped what they were doing to watch me being escorted at gunpoint through their sleepy town. We came to a fork in the road and I craned my neck to see where they wanted me to go. Randall pointed to the right with his rifle. As I got around a bend, I saw the American camp spread out in front of me. I stopped in my tracks. While I was concerned for my safety, my mouth hung open at the sight of my countrymen. As I was soaking in the sight, one of the soldiers pushed me in the back with his musket. I went scrambling forward, barely avoiding falling face-first onto the road.

We entered the camp and the soldier, whose name I didn't know, walked ahead. He got into an animated conversation with a young Lieutenant. He jerked a thumb in my direction and the officer looked over his shoulder at me. I watched intently as the young man strode in my direction.

"I'm told that you claim to be a Colonel in the continental regulars. Why aren't you in uniform?"

I snapped at him. "Like I told the soldier, I was taken prisoner when Charleston fell to the British. I escaped but had to change clothes to escape the area. Lieutenant, take me to General Greene. He knows me."

My outburst had the desired results. The Lieutenant looked as if I had offended him and turned. "Follow me." I stepped in behind him and watched with some amusement as my captors laughed at my treatment of the officer. We passed rows of canvas tents until we came to the largest one. Command headquarters. As we got to the tent, the flap opened and out stepped Nathanael Green and Jonathon Taylor. I took a deep breath.

"Colonel Smith, it is you."

I stood at attention and saluted. "General Greene, good to see you." My eyes pivoted to Taylor. He shrugged his shoulders.

Greene returned my salute and dismissed the young officer. "Come in my tent. We have much to discuss."

I followed him into the large and spacious tent. A table in the middle had a map spread out on it showing the colony of South Carolina. There were other ranking officers standing around the table studying the map. They looked up as we entered. "Gentlemen, this is Colonel Peter Smith. You may have heard about his exploits in the Navy sinking a large British frigate." There were a few nods and some looks of astonishment. I looked down, not wanting the attention.

General Greene took a better look at me. "My God, Smith. What did the British do to you?"

My cheeks reddened as everyone in the tent stared at me. "It was quite an unpleasant experience being locked away in a darkened dungeon and left to die."

"Are you fit for duty?"

"Yes, sir. If you will have me."

He just stood there inspecting me. He looked like he was weighing the idea of allowing me to serve or send me home. "Very well, Colonel," He turned to the map and pointed at our location. "We are still consolidating the Army. I have decided to split our forces and send half the men under General Morgan." He pointed out the large man with wide shoulders. Morgan nodded at me. "He will take his forces to the northwest to bring the British out in the open. I will take the other half south and try to envelop them in a trap. Gentlemen, we are going to take this colony back and destroy the enemy." He banged the table with his fist.

He spent the next hour detailing the plan. I felt fortunate to be involved in the discussions. I still didn't know what my role would be. After the General finished he dismissed everyone except General Morgan and me.

"Colonel, I want you to go with General Morgan and command one of his regiments. I know your record and knowledge of military tactics. I also know of your bravery under fire." General Morgan looked at my missing arm. "You will be in good hands with Daniel."

"Thank you, sir, for the opportunity to serve."

"We will leave in a couple of days. We need to get you a proper uniform and meal."

Chapter 72

Nigel Crittenden

Bring Up Your Men

We got an early start the next morning. The weather had turned colder. I welcomed the change from the heat and humidity. I had a good feeling that we would catch up with Colonel Tarleton today. I was troubled about the damage that we witnessed along the way. This was certainly not how gentlemen conduct a war. I would reserve judgment until I was able to speak with the Colonel to hear his side.

I pushed the men hard. We needed to reach the main body. I felt exposed out here in the open. It might not bode well if we run into a sizable number of Rebels. Another benefit of speeding the men up was keeping them warm to combat the icy feel of the winter air. The downfall would be halting the march and the men freezing from the sweat they built up under their frocks. There was a sense of destiny in this campaign. I felt that we were on the verge of total victory.

Around noon, I heard the distinct sound of dozens of horses thundering down the road ahead of us. I turned to the men and told them to take a break while I rode ahead. I took off, putting my horse into a gallop. Up ahead I heard shouts and the sound of gunfire. I pulled back on the reins.

Should I go back and bring up the men? I decided to cautiously go toward the sound of fighting first.

The road took a sharp turn to the left. The sound of gunfire started to slacken. When I turned the corner, I saw British soldiers and horsemen forming a line to go into the woods in front of them. Glancing down, bodies lay in the road. I spotted an officer and rode in his direction. The man was shouting orders from atop his horse. He had a jaunty-looking helmet on his head topped by a black feather. Must be Tarleton. He noticed me and tilted his head.

"Who are you, Lieutenant?"

"Nigel Crittenden," I answered, snapping off a salute. He tried to look around me for others. "Where is your command?"

I turned and pointed behind me.

He yelled out, "We are under attack. Go bring up your men." Off he rode. I turned the horse around and went back to my men. I ordered them to double time to assist in the battle that could still be heard. When we reached the treeline, I could see that Tarleton's men had completed their attack and returned to the roadway. My men spread out into a single line and were prepared for an attack that did not come.

Tarleton sauntered his horse in my direction. "Just a band of militia. They got off a few volleys before melting into the woods. We killed a few of them, but the others got away." He looked at my squad of men. "Is this all you brought with you?"

"Yes, sir. We were ordered to join up with your command by General Cornwallis."

He fidgeted in the saddle. "Very well. We will camp here tonight. See to your men and put out pickets in case the Rebels try to attack again."

I roamed the camp that night trying to get a sense of Tarleton's purpose in using his command to accomplish total warfare. I needed to know why the war was being taken to civilians. I had to be cautious in my inquiries. I noted that the men were in good spirits even after the attack today that led to six deaths and a dozen wounded. There was loud boasting about whipping the Rebels and ending the war. Morale was vital to the success of any army. Were these men too confident?

I came across three junior officers sitting around a campfire passing a flask among themselves. By the look of their uniforms, they were infantry, not cavalry. One of the group noticed me and motioned me over with his arm. "Lieutenant, come join us."

I sat down on a fallen tree trunk and stared into the fire. Another young man passed me the flask. "Haven't seen you before. Names Reynolds, welcome to the party."

I nodded. "Crittenden. We arrived today." I took a sip of the bitter-tasting liquid. I struggled to hold back a cough. "We have been chasing you for a few days. It wasn't hard to find you just had to follow the burning structures." All three of them laughed.

"Colonel Tarleton likes his fires. He thinks it's the best way to put down the rebellion." He snatched the flask from me. "Names Asbury. That is Miller." He said pointing to the third officer. Miller nodded at me. I threw another log on the fire and it blazed. "Do you know what the mission of this command is?"

Reynolds looked at his fellow Lieutenants. "Our orders are to destroy any possible Rebel threat and remove all enemy resistance from the colony. At least that is what Tarleton tells us."

I hesitated but asked. "Does that include targeting innocent civilians?"

Asbury spoke up. "You haven't been here long, have you? These people aren't so innocent. They are just as bad as the so-called Continental Army."

He pointed to the other two men. "We all command a company of loyalist soldiers. All these men want to do is take revenge against their neighbors for perceived wrongs they have committed. It's a nasty business. We just follow orders and try not to think about it."

Miller piped up and raised the flask. "Enough gloom, gentlemen. Happy New Year."

I had quite forgotten, it was now 1781.

Chapter 73

Anne Smith

Back on the Road

It's been a week since Peter left. There has been no word from him. I debated what to do since he left. I go back and forth. Do I try to follow him again, stay here and wait, or take Beatrice and go home? I remember with some shame my last words to my husband. I deeply love him, but I can't turn a blind eye to his actions. He seems to have a death wish. I can't continually forgive him for abandoning us. At least at home, there are my parents and the Smiths. I made up my mind. I will go home. How do I get there? Peter took our horse and my funds are limited. I understand the risk of traveling during the winter with British soldiers roaming all over. My other dilemma is the pending birth of our second child.

I have befriended some of the locals in the hopes that they can help me escape this place and get back to Cambridge. Asking around about transportation to Boston, the consensus was to get to the coast and take passage on a ship up north. That would be easier said than done during a war, in the winter with a baby expected at any time. It's unclear if the British still commanded all of the coastal area since they captured Charleston. The smart choice would be to wait it out until after having the baby. I am past that now. I needed to go now.

I made arrangements with the innkeeper to be allowed to get transportation from Chester to Camden on a supply train that regularly passed through taking supplies to the various British forts in the area. He told me that some of the drivers stayed at the inn and had become friends. After reaching Camden, I would need to find a way back to Charleston and somehow talk or bribe my way on a ship that traveled north. Sounded too good to be true. Still, I had to try.

The innkeeper took pity on us and refunded some of what Peter paid for our stay. He also packed a bag with dried beef, rice, biscuits and coffee that should last for a while. I had been blessed by people such as this man along the way who were willing to help. The night before I was to leave, Mr. Stewart introduced me to the driver. A man named Wilson. We talked over a meal in the darkened lower floor of the inn. The man was disagreeable, filthy and profane. I had a sense of dread trusting my life and the lives of my children to him. He eyed me as he shoveled spoonfuls of stew into his mouth. Then he absently wiped off his mouth with his sleeve.

"Mr. Stewart told me that you need passage to Camden."

"Yes, sir. For me and my daughter."

He looked at Beatrice who was sitting next to me eating her dinner. "Are you sure you want to travel this time of year? It's not safe out there." He peered over the table at my expanding stomach.

I held back the fit of anger that I felt. "I need to get us away from all the fighting that's going on to protect my child...children."

He pursed his lips and nodded. I looked around and then slid the small purse over to him. He picked it up and weighed the contents with his hand. "Be ready to leave at dawn."

Bright and early the next morning we were on our way. There was a line of ten wagons filled with supplies confiscated from the surrounding farms to provision the British troops billeted in Camden. Mr. Wilson had carved out a space for me and Beatrice among the supplies. It somewhat protected us from the elements but we had to put on layers of clothes and blankets to stay warm. I watched Beatrice and wondered how all this was affecting her. She was such a good child and endured more than anyone should. My eyes welled with tears thinking about the hardships we faced in the past and those ahead.

The going was slow; it took two days to reach Camden. We were dropped off before arriving at the British fort that was set up on the edge of town. Wilson suggested that we take a room in town to get a hot meal and find transportation to Charleston. He warned against trusting any of the redcoats.

There was a break in the weather and it was a sunny and warm January day. I held Beatrice's hand and walked alongside the road leading into town. The British presence was everywhere. We received a few looks as we walked, but no one stopped us. At the edge of town, there was a boarding house. It was run by a woman named Polly McAllister. She took one look at us and ushered us into her parlor.

"What are you doing out by yourself? Are you in trouble?"

I looked around the house while she threw questions at me. It was a nice home like ours back in Cambridge. When Polly stopped talking, I started to answer, but Beatrice spoke up. "Mommy, why are we here? Where is Daddy?"

I bent down and picked her up. "Daddy is away. We are trying to get home."

Polly's mouth hung open. "Please come in and warm up by the fire. Let me get you something to eat. I started to unwrap Beatrice and we sat on a couch that was the most comfortable thing I had sat on in weeks. A few minutes later, Polly came into the room holding a tray. She sat it down and sat across from me in a chair. I could tell that she was trying to think how to ask me about Peter. I beat her to the punch.

"My husband is an officer in the Continental Army. He's somewhere trying to get back into the war after escaping from Charleston." I picked up a biscuit from the tray and stuffed it in my mouth. Polly sat speechless. I finished chewing the biscuit. "It feels good to get that off my chest. I don't know where your loyalties lie, Mrs. McAllister, but I've had enough of this war. I'm trying to take my daughter back to my home in Massachusetts."

She sat back in the chair. "What can I do to help?"

"I'm told the best way to get to Boston is to get to Charleston and catch a ship. I need to get to Charleston the safest way possible. I also need to make sure that this one comes into this world without being on the road." I moved the blanket off my belly.

Polly stared at the huge hump. "Oh my. When are you due?"

I rubbed my bulging midsection. "Any day now. I was wondering if I could stay here until then?"

She stood up. "Of course, you can stay here. You are safe. My husband was killed by the British. I will protect you from those monsters."

Chapter 74

Peter Smith

Cowpens

I felt refreshed and invigorated to be back in the heat of the action. I looked over at the uniform that I was provided. A gift from our French allies. It made everything real. It was blue with a white collar and lapel lined with golden buttons. I wore the silver epaulets denoting my rank. I was still gaunt and frail but it made me feel ten feet tall. I had to be the man I was before my time spent in the dungeon in Charleston. It would take more than wearing a uniform for that to happen.

There was an energy in the camp that could be felt. The men were ready to turn the tide against the British. This was to be the catalyst for us to rid the Redcoats from South Carolina and ultimately earn our independence after so many years of struggle. I rose from my cot and emerged from the tent to a frigid morning. The camp was coming alive and I ambled over to get a cup of coffee and something to eat.

General Morgan called the officers for a briefing. I chewed on a stale biscuit and followed the others to Morgan's tent. There were brief greetings then the General got down to business. He was as animated as I had ever seen him. The deadly game we played with our enemy was about to get serious. We surrounded a crude map of the area.

"Our scouts have placed the main body of Redcoats heading our way. We are camped here at Burr's Mill." He pointed to the map. "I have already dispatched Colonel Pickets and his militia to this road junction at Cowpens." I leaned in to get a better look. "Tarleton has grown overconfident by his "victories" over the townspeople of South Carolina. Men, this is our opportunity to use his arrogance to defeat him. We will march to Cowpens and give Tarleton a welcome he will never forget."

We broke camp and were on the road. I rode forward mulling General Morgan's words. He planned to create a trap that the British would walk into and be destroyed piecemeal. As part of the plan, he intended to use militia to make a stand against the main line of British infantry. These men were typically skittish and tended to flee after seeing the might of the enemy. Morgan was counting on this and ordered that they fire at least two volleys before retreating. The general believed that Tarleton's arrogance would force him to engage the bulk of his command to chase after them. Then the American regulars would envelop and crush the unaware Redcoats. I was to assist in leading a regiment of regulars from Delaware, Maryland and Virginia commanded by Lieutenant Colonel John Howard. We were to be placed directly behind the first line of militia. God help the British when they come up against us. The plan was sound, in theory. I know how plans can change in the heat of battle.

Colonel Howard and I discussed our role in the upcoming fight as we rode down that country path. I had not had the privilege to meet him before. I was instantly impressed by his demeanor and his leadership qualities. He indicated that he was from Maryland and had certainly heard of me and my exploits. "Colonel, everyone in the north has heard what you did on Breed's Hill and against the British ship. It is an honor to serve with you."

I hated to have any accolades thrown my way and changed the subject. "Do you think this ruse will work? Are they so confident that they would fall for this trap?"

He cocked his head in my direction. "Are these not the same officers that continued to charge your line on Breed's Hill only to be cut down until you ran out of ammunition?"

We marched southeast down the Green River Road and reached our destination mid-afternoon. The area seemed perfect for a trap. There was a narrow clearing surrounded by trees on three sides and a river on one end. The militia had camped at the northwest end of the field. I noticed there was great concealment from trees and hills behind the militia where the bulk of the Army would remain hidden. A detachment of Continental cavalry was posted to the north of the intended battlefield.

General Morgan ordered a herd of cattle to be slaughtered to feed the men and we settled down to wait for the British. I walked among the men to introduce myself and check their morale as they sat by their fires eating fresh beef. These men from the mid-Atlantic were jovial and talkative. This was a good sign that they were prepared to perform their duty. They also had full bellies and were content to wait for the British. We were stationed on the left side behind the inexperienced militia. I had seen for myself how these untrained men had reacted under fire in the past. Rumor was that General Morgan himself had given these men from the Carolinas a pep talk about how the Redcoats had destroyed their property and harmed their families. Let's pray that they make a stand.

I had trouble falling asleep that night. I lay on the frozen ground and stared up at the stars in the sky. Growing up in the city had not given me a true appreciation of the beauty of the heavens. I shuddered to keep warm. Civilized men should not fight in these conditions. The thought gave me pause. I suppose we could go into winter camp again and this war would drag on and on.

I must have dozed off and was awoken by the sound of movement. I sat up and witnessed a pinkish glow off to the east as the sun was making its daily appearance. Men were scurrying into place. I grabbed my sword and stood. I stopped a soldier who was rushing past me. "What is happening, soldier?"

His eyes were wide with fear as he noticed me. "Colonel, the British are on the field."

"Very well. Take your place."

The men took up their positions. I went to find Colonel Howard. He was pacing behind the men barking orders. He motioned for me. "Colonel, I put you in charge of our left line. Remember that we are to hold our position after the militia has fled to our rear. We are positioned about one hundred and fifty yards behind them. From our vantage point below this rise, the British line won't know that we are here prepared to accept their charge. We will make them pay."

I nodded and ran off to the left. The men were already in place. They knew what to do. I tried to look through the line to see any sign of the enemy. All I could see was the uneven ranks of militia. I tried to stand on the tips of my toes. Still could not see them. It was just a waiting game now. I held my sword tightly and paced behind the men encouraging them.

Then out of nowhere came the crashing sound of hundreds of muskets going off. A moan went up in our front and shouts could be heard. I tensed up waiting for what would happen next. Another uneven echo of musket fire came next. Then out of the corner of my eye, I saw the militia running off to the left to go around our line.

Our turn next.

Chapter 75

Nigel Crittenden

The One-Armed Man

W e rose early the next morning at 2 o'clock and were on the march by 3. There was frost on the ground and it was dark. I scanned the early morning sky. It was crisp and clear, dotted by millions of blinking stars. The moon was setting and was only about half visible. There wouldn't be much light to guide our way. I was concerned that the men had not gotten enough rest. Orders were orders. I had been assigned to lead a company of Light Infantry. There had not been any time to get acquainted with the men. I had no idea of how they would fight when the time came. We marched in columns north. I was chilled by the frozen air and not knowing what lay ahead.

I was aware that we had over a thousand men to face whatever the rebels would put up against us. We had superior numbers in cavalry and artillery that could defeat any resistance we faced. I should be confident, but something told me this would be a difficult day. We had been marching for hours and off to my right I saw the early light from the rising sun. There was a reddish glow through the woods. Did this portend a possible disaster? As the scenery became clearer, we were halted awaiting orders. Then the command came to deploy. We had entered a narrow field that was surrounded by trees. It was the perfect place to defend. I barked out orders for the men to line up to the right in lines two deep to prepare for a frontal attack. The men fixed bayonets to the end of their rifles. I squinted trying to see what we were facing. I was perhaps ten yards in front of the men and could see the faint outline of rebels in loose formation directly to our front. It couldn't be, they were militia. I swiveled my head to the left. There were a few hundred men facing us. As we closed the distance, shots rang out from the Rebel line. There were gaps opened in our lines as men were hit. A few men returned fire. Fools, they are out of range. I yelled back, "Hold your fire," and raised my sword to continue the advance.

When we got within a few hundred yards, there came a second volley. The air was ripe with the sound of musket balls passing and the field was covered in smoke. There was a terrible tug on my left shoulder. It felt as if I was punched and it pushed my back. I looked down and saw blood spurt out of my coat. I've been wounded. There wasn't much pain and I continued the attack. I did not look back to see how many men had fallen. When we closed the gap, the men stopped and released a volley at the escaping militia.

We followed the enemy over a rise prepared to finish them off. As I crested the ridge, I gasped and felt utter horror. Aligned before me were lines of regulars. Before I could even react, the enemy line erupted in fire. The screams of my men could be heard above the din. I was untouched by this volley and continued. The few men I had still standing returned fire, and then we continued into the hailstorm of rifle fire. As some of the smoke cleared from the field, I caught a glimpse of an American officer rallying his men. I blinked in disbelief. The man was missing an arm. "Smith!"

I was oblivious to my wound and went on as if driven by some evil force. I could sense reinforcements were filling the gaps in the line and I saw the dragoons charge past on my right. I remained focused on that singular figure who was the reason I was here. There continued to be sporadic gunfire from both sides and the Americans began to back away. There were yells from our line and we followed them.

The one-armed man continued to lead his men and suddenly he was down. No, he is mine. I hurried my pace ignoring the men around me. When I got to the spot where I saw him fall, he was gone. I halted and frantically searched around me. The fighting was intense, but I would not be stopped in my quest. To my dismay, there was another fresh line of rebels lined up to stop us. I nearly tumbled to the ground knowing all was lost, when I spotted Smith again. He had somehow made it to the line of defenders.

I made up my mind, if I was to die today it would be after I killed the man who caused my father's death. I raised my sword high above my head and started running forward. The rest of the world was blanked out as bullets flew by me. I reached the American line and swung my sword wildly at the line of Americans. Smith's eyes locked on me and he tilted his head. With every ounce of strength I had left, I screamed, "Smith come and fight me. You killed my father." Just as he came closer, my world went blank.

Chapter 76

Peter Smith

The Meeting

The militia did their duty. I yelled out, "Ready men, the Redcoats will be coming over that rise. Prepare to fire." Through the blanket of smoke came a ragged line of the enemy. I noticed the bayonets first. It made me think back to that charge against us on Breed's Hill. On the enemy soldiers came maintaining discipline. We opened up a deadly volley and it punched gaps in the lines of red-coated troops. Even though they were the hated enemy, I still had to admire their bravery as they closed up the gaps and continued their advance.

I saw through the haze of battle that replacements were coming up to assist the first line. I rallied the men to continue the fight. The pressure from the attacking force began to be too much and the line began a slow organized retreat. I encouraged the men to keep up a steady fire. I moved among them waving my sword. I could feel it start to collapse and knew that there was another line behind us. As I yelled out, "Retreat in good order men," I felt a sting at my side and I couldn't keep my footing. I tumbled to the ground. Not again. I felt around to see where I was wounded. Reaching inside my coat, I felt around. The hot sensation of blood could be felt on my right hand. I pulled the hand out, it was covered with crimson.

I watched the men retreat from their positions. I couldn't stay here and be captured. Slowly, as my head spun, I dragged myself up on my feet. A glance over my shoulder told me the British were close. I steadied my legs and half stooped over, and raced for friendly lines. I felt hands grab me and pull me through the line to relative safety. I bent over catching my breath and tested the pain on my side. My head began to clear and I could stand.

I looked up in time to see a massed volley being fired by the American line in front of me. The stench of gunpowder drifted over me. I coughed trying to clear my lungs. Desperately peering through the line, I tried to see the damage done to the enemy. I gasped at the number of red-clad bodies piled in our front. Then movement caught my attention. It was a British officer with his sword waving over his head. He was running toward our line. I noticed the spreading stain of blood on his shoulder. Still, he came. Then the strangest thing happened. I could hear him scream, "Smith, you killed my father!" I had no idea what he was talking about.

I watched with fascination as the young man made it to our lines only to be struck in the head by a musket. I couldn't take my eyes off him as his body dropped to the ground motionless. My attention then returned to the battle. The men kept up a steady fire and eventually, the British line broke and retreated to the rear. The roar of a cheer went up from the American line. I had no idea what was happening on the rest of the field, but I knew that we won our part of the battle.

My wound was dressed and found not to be life-threatening. I was told that we had achieved a great victory and the British were in full retreat, but not before we had exacted severe casualties to their ranks. I wondered what happened to that young British officer who called out my name. I had to find out. Against the wishes of the surgeon, I went back to my part of the battlefield to find him. I had fought in many battles and had seen what war could do to a man. Still, I was overcome by the sight of all those dead men still lying on the field. I gingerly made my way to our position and carefully looked through the heaps of dead.

After searching each of the nameless casualties, I decided that he was not there. My next move was to go to all the aid stations that were set up to care for the wounded. I truly wished that the young man survived so that I could talk to him. I was disappointed at each place I searched until someone told me that the British wounded officers were being treated at the church in town. I couldn't give up now and headed in that direction. When I got outside the small church, I was stopped by a guard. He looked at my blood-covered coat and my empty sleeve. "Colonel, we are not allowing anyone to talk to the prisoners."

I reached out and patted him on his shoulder. "You will need to shoot me, Private, to prevent my entrance. I am on a mission to see the man that called out my name on the battlefield."

He looked to see if I was serious, then moved out of my way. I entered the church and was overcome by the stench of death and the moans from the wounded. Men were laid out on the pews while surgeons tended to them. Blood covered the wooden floor. I walked slowly among the rows of benches trying to find him. I gritted my teeth and would not be deterred. As I reached the rear of the church, I saw him sitting in the corner propped against a pew, his legs splayed out in front of him. He had a large bandage over his head and shoulder.

I walked over without him noticing me. "How do you know me?"

The wounded man suddenly looked up at me and gasped. "It's you."

"Who are you?"

He tried to stand but fell back in a heap. "You are responsible for my father dying."

I was more confused than ever. "Who was your father?"

"Ambrose Crittenden."

A vision struck me. "Oh, I see." I sat down on the pew across from him. "Your father was an honorable man. I respected him. He was one of the few men on that ship that I did."

He looked confused. "Then why did you kill him?"

I took a deep breath. "I didn't kill your father. I don't know who told you that. There was much confusion that day, but I never saw him when we captured the Progress."

His face was contorted in agony and I pitied him. "It can't be.... It was you."

I shook my head no. "Is that why you are here?"

"I made it my life's mission to avenge his death. I have been trying to find you for years."

I leaned closer. "Trust me, killing someone for vengeance won't make things better for you. I should know."

He lowered his head. "What will happen to me now?"

"I suppose that you will be a prisoner until the war is over. I pray for both of our sake that will be soon. Then maybe you can go home and get on with your life." I stood and took one more look at him and left.

Chapter 77

Anne Smith

It's a Boy

I screamed out. The pain was unbearable. My breathing was sporadic as I waited for the next round of contractions. The perspiration poured off my face and into my eyes. I tried to focus on who was around me. Polly summoned a midwife when my water broke. She sat patiently keeping watch over the delivery. She said soothing words that were lost on me. I suddenly thought of Beatrice and looked around the small bedroom for her. "Where is my daughter?"

A voice from behind me said, "She is next door with Mrs. Johnson. She is safe."

I strained my neck to see who said that. I focused on the smiling face of Mrs. McAllister. She placed a damp cloth on my forehead. Everyone was so calm. Except for me. I needed my mother more than at any time in my life. It had not been this difficult when I gave birth to Beatrice. My eyes rolled back in my head when the next set of cramps set in. The midwife, I don't recall her name, ordered, "Breathe. It will help with the pain."

I blinked the sweat from my eyes and started to breathe in and out trying to concentrate. I instantly had the urge to push. I grabbed handfuls of the bedding and bore down.

"Wait! Don't push yet. The baby has turned."

I was alarmed by the tone of her voice. The pain became secondary now. Will my baby survive this? I felt strong hands pushing on my stomach.

"I will try to turn the baby so that their head is down. You mustn't push right now."

Mrs. McAllister took one of my hands in hers and leaned closer to me. "You are doing great, Anne. Keep breathing and focus on the baby, not the pain." The need to push came on stronger and I had to squeeze Polly's hand to fight the urge. The midwife pressed down trying to maneuver the baby. After a few minutes, she declared, "The baby's head has crowned. You can start pushing during the next cramp."

I didn't have long to wait. I pushed with all my might and started to feel numb down there. When the cramp stopped, I stopped pushing.

"Don't stop now! The head is coming out."

I sucked in a deep breath and started pushing again.

"The head is out. Oh my. Mrs. Smith. The cord is wrapped around the baby's neck. You have to push as hard as you can. Now!"

I screamed and pushed. I nearly passed out from the exertion. There was no sound from the midwife or the baby. My eyes desperately searched Polly's face for a sign. There was terror in her eyes and she avoided looking at me. "What's wrong with my baby? Polly tell me."

She looked at me. "The baby is blue."

I heard movement. Then the sound of the midwife slapping the baby. "Breathe baby, breathe."

Both hands flew to my face and I started to bawl uncontrollably. This war had taken so much from me and now my baby. I felt the comforting arms of Polly and she cried along with me. Then came the sweetest sound in the world, the baby started wailing. The midwife came into view cleaning up my baby with a towel. She came over and placed the baby on my chest. "Mrs. Smith, you have a baby boy."

The birthing ordeal drained every amount of energy that I had. I was bedridden for three days. Only awoken to nurse the baby. The baby. Peter and I had not decided on a name. Events overtook us and now he was off somewhere fighting the British. It had been a few weeks and I had not heard from him. I was still angry at him for leaving me in this state. My plan to make it home before the baby came also didn't work out.

I had three days to think about what I would do next. It was in the middle of winter and I was too weak to travel alone with two children. Mrs. McAllister told me that we could stay as long as we wanted. I think that she enjoyed our company. She was especially close to Beatrice as she didn't have any children of her own.

Lately, there had been strange actions by the British troops stationed in Camden. They seemed to be skittish and even less friendly than before. Rumors were rampant in town of a stunning defeat by the American Army. We hoped that they would leave and we could go on with our lives.

I sat down and wrote letters to Peter telling him about our son but mostly appealing to him to come to get me and take us back to Boston. The problem was not knowing where to send them. Polly went into town each day to try and get any news on the whereabouts of the Army and any sign of a British withdrawal. Most days she would come back and just shake her head. Then on a Saturday, she came through the front door excitedly squealing as she found me in my bedroom feeding the baby.

"Anne, you will never guess what news I just heard."

I was amused by her energy and just twisted my head waiting for her to tell me.

She sat on the bed next to me and caught her breath. "The British are packing up to leave. I heard them say they were going to North Carolina and that the Rebels defeated an army commanded by Colonel Tarleton somewhere west of here. They were concerned about what would happen to them. Isn't that the greatest news?"

I sat there digesting her words. My thoughts went to Peter. "Did they say anything about casualties?" I saw the change of expression on her face.

"They didn't say, only indicated that they suffered a crushing defeat and were retreating out of South Carolina."

I put the baby over my shoulder to burp. "Maybe Peter will finally come to me so we can leave this place."

Chapter 78

Peter Smith

You Have Done Enough

My wound became infected and I ran a high fever for a few days. While I slept in my tent, there was a lot of activity around camp. General Morgan came to see me personally. My fever had broken, but I was still having trouble focusing. He took a seat next to my cot and had a troubled look on his face.

"Colonel, are you well?"

I propped myself up. "General, I apologize for my absence."

He reached over and patted my shoulder. "I came to see how you are feeling. I heard about your bravery on the field and wanted to thank you before I leave."

I blinked my eyes. "Where are you going?"

He smirked. "I have decided that I am used up. I plan on going home to Virginia. I felt it was my duty to come back to the Army after the debacle at Camden. It's time for me to go home."

My mouth hung open. "What will happen now?"

He stood up. "I have received reports that the British have retreated into North Carolina. General Greene has taken the Army and is chasing after him."

I tried to slowly sit up and became dizzy. He reached out to steady me. I held up my hand and he backed off. "General, what is to become of me?"

"Colonel, it's your choice, but I think you have done enough. Go home and take care of your family." He opened the tent flap letting in sunlight and was gone.

I blinked at the blinding rays on my face. I was troubled by the general's words. *Had I done enough?* I sat on my cot and thought back to all that I had experienced from being taken from my home in England until this moment. All the death that I had seen. Then the promise that I made and broke with Anne to go back to Boston. Maybe I had done enough.

I looked around my small tent and saw some papers on the bedside table. I gingerly reached over to see what they were. It was a stack of letters. My pulse increased and my hand trembled as I opened the first one. I had difficulty focusing on the page, but my eyebrows raised as I scanned her words. My arm absently came down to my side and I dropped the letter to the ground. The baby arrived and it's a boy. Anne indicated that she was in Camden and needed me. I was in shock. I didn't leave under good conditions and I expected her to go back to Boston. Now I find out that she is near and the baby...a boy...has been born.

I quickly concluded that I would find her and take her home. This time I knew that I would fulfill my promise. I swiveled my head around the cramped tent. I won't have much to pack. I needed to leave today. First things first. I needed to find someone in charge to resign my commission and arrange transportation. I walked out into the sunlight. There was chaos all around me as the men were packing up the camp preparing to join up with General Greene in his advance north to defeat the British. I stood transfixed by the scene. I noticed a young lieutenant striding in front of me. "Lieutenant."

The young man looked in my direction and I beckoned him with my arm. He looked around him and turned my way. He acted as if I were going to chastise him. "Can I assist you, Colonel?"

"Can you direct me to the officer in charge?"

"Colonel Howard is over there." He pointed off to the north at the edge of the woods. I nodded and headed that way. The world came into focus as I neared the colonel. "Colonel Howard, can I speak with you?"

He was standing in front of his tent talking to some other officers. "Colonel Smith, good to see you up and about." He must have noticed the concern on my face. "Certainly. We can step into my tent." I followed him with my hat in my hand. "Is there something I can help you with?"

I avoided eye contact. I had a hard time getting the nerve to ask him for my leave. After a few awkward moments, I cleared my throat. "Colonel, I just found out that my wife gave birth to a baby boy."

Howard came over to me and patted me on the back. "Congratulations are in order, Colonel."

"Thank you, sir." I began to sweat and shifted from one leg to the other. "What I wanted to talk to you about...umm...I would like to resign my commission and take my family back home."

Colonel Howard took a step back and considered my request. "You are a fine officer and I will miss you. I will have the papers drawn up and you can be on your way." He extended his hand. I put my hat on and shook his hand.

An hour later I was on the road on a horse that was provided for me. That was the hardest thing that I've had to do, resigning my commission. I knew it was the right decision, but walking away from the war before it was decided went against all my beliefs. Riding in silence, I considered what I would do next. I guess I could go back and run my father's business. That would provide for a good life for us. How could it possibly compare to all the adventures I had experienced?

Chapter 79

Anne Smith

I'm Back for Good

I slowly regained my strength after the difficult delivery. It had been a few weeks and the baby was healthy. He cried a lot and was often hungry. I had a hard time keeping up with his feeding schedule. I was so grateful for Mrs. McAllister through all this. She helped with Beatrice and took turns with the baby. The baby, what would we name him? I was holding off hoping that Peter would find us and we could name him together. I had not heard from Peter since he left. There was so much hope after hearing of the great victory over the British, but no word of casualties. I had sent a slew of letters. It was impossible to know if they reached him.

I was awoken from a shallow sleep by a tree limb banging against the window of my upstairs bedroom. I sat up and looked at the crib praying that the noise hadn't stirred the baby. He was still sleeping. I yawned and stretched. Pulling myself from the bed, I took a glance at the mirror on the dresser. I looked aghast. I pulled a brush through my unruly hair and went to go downstairs to check on Beatrice. As I pulled open the door, I heard a loud squeal. Nearly panicking, I ran down the stairs thinking that something was wrong.

When I reached the bottom step, I noticed a man was standing inside the front door. He was holding Beatrice. He wore tattered and filthy clothes. His hair was matted down and there was a growth of whiskers on his face. I was about to scream at the man to put down my daughter when I got a better look at his face. "Peter!"

He gently put Beatrice down and walked to me. "I'm back for good." He engulfed me in a hug and I melted crying with joy. I had so many questions, but couldn't release him in fear he would be a mirage. Beatrice pulled at my dress. "Daddy is home."

I looked into his tired eyes. "Yes, he is." I noticed that Mrs. McAllister was standing off to the side watching the events unfold. "Mrs. McAllister, this is my husband Peter." She smiled and slightly bowed. "It's good to finally meet you, Mr. Smith." Peter returned the bow. "Thank you, Mrs. McAllister, for taking care of my family." He then looked around the room. "Where is the baby?"

Before I could open my mouth, a cry came from upstairs. "He's up there."

Peter smiled and climbed the stairs. A few minutes later, he returned with the baby cradled in his arm. "He's perfect. What have you named him?"

I took the baby. It was time to feed him. "I was waiting for you to come home to name him." I started to walk to another room for privacy. "Why don't you get cleaned up and we can decide on a name after I feed him." I could hear Mrs. McAllister directing Peter to the kitchen where she would prepare a bath for him. While the baby fed, I thought, *this is all I wanted for our family to be reunited.*

We talked at length about what name should be given to the baby. I argued for Peter Junior. Peter fought against this as he wanted the boy to be his own man. He suggested we name him after his adoptive father John. I knew that would be a great honor for his parents, but it didn't seem right to me. I asked Peter who he most respected. He thought about it for a few minutes and answered, "George Washington." It was settled, George Washington Smith.

Chapter 80

Peter Smith

Wait to Go Home

Winter turned into spring and we received word that the American Army pushed the British out of North Carolina into Virginia. This gave us hope that the war was nearing its end. Mrs. McAllister was a gracious host and seemed to enjoy that we were staying with her. I longed to leave and go back to Boston. We were destined to be stuck in Camden for now. The war still raged to the north of us and Charleston was still in British hands. We also had two small children to consider. Our best bet was to catch passage on a ship from a southern port. Going through Charleston or Savannah was just too risky.

I felt worthless not having anything to do with my time. We still had some money, but after paying rent to Mrs. McAllister we needed to save for passage to Boston. I tried my hand at odd jobs around Camden, but there was not much for a one-armed man to do. Out of pity, I was offered work in an office as an accountant due to my experience in my father's trade business. The work was tedious and I only worked part time.

Reading the reports in the local newspaper about the progress of the war was hard on me. A part of me longed for the adventure and action that made me feel alive. However, when these thoughts entered my mind,

I would think about my family and my vow. It was a joy to spend time with my children. I would give them the life that I was denied.

Now we wait to go home.

To follow the continuing exploits of Peter and Anne Smith, get your copy of Book 3 in The Peter Smith Chronicles series, THE REGRETS OF MEN. https://www.amazon.com/Regrets-Men-Sequel-Sacrifices-Chronicles-ebook/dp/B0D46SJ83H

To my mother Bobby and step-mother Pauline. You have had a strong influence on me and my creative abilities. I would also like to thank David Roberts for proofreading and editing this undertaking.

About the Author

Dan Bradbury is originally from Colorado. He is retired from a career working in the insurance industry. He also served in the U.S. Navy. Dan has a life long interest in history and story telling. He currently lives in South Carolina with his wife Tricia.

Please leave your review of *The Sacrifices of Men* on www.amazon.com, www.goodreads.com, and www.bookbub.com.

Also By

By Danny J. Bradbury

A Common Man

The Sins of Men

From the Plains to the Sea